CHOOSE YOUR OWN
ADULTHOOD

CHOOSE YOUR OWN
ADULTHOOD

A SMALL BOOK ABOUT THE SMALL CHOICES THAT MAKE THE BIGGEST DIFFERENCE

HAL RUNKEL

FOREWORD BY HANNAH RUNKEL

GREENLEAF
BOOK GROUP PRESS

Published by Greenleaf Book Group Press
Austin, Texas
www.gbgpress.com

Distributed by Greenleaf Book Group
For ordering information or special discounts for bulk purchases, please contact
Greenleaf Book Group at PO Box 91869, Austin, TX 78709, 512.891.6100.

Design and composition by Greenleaf Book Group and Kim Lance
Cover design by Greenleaf Book Group and Kim Lance

Cataloging-in-Publication data is available.

Print ISBN: 978-1-62634-352-8
eBook ISBN: 978-1-62634-384-9

Part of the Tree Neutral® program, which offsets the number of trees
consumed in the production and printing of this book by taking
proactive steps, such as planting trees in direct proportion to the number
of trees used: www.treeneutral.com

Printed in the United States of America on acid-free paper
16 17 18 19 20 21   10 9 8 7 6 5 4 3 2 1
First Edition

To my daughter,
Hannah.

This book was originally written to you,
and
I thank you for allowing me to share it with the world.

You're such a strong young adult already;
I'm just so glad I get to know you . . .
and love you.

It is our choices . . . that show what we truly are,
far more than our abilities.

—J.K. ROWLING

CONTENTS

Hi. My name is Hannah Runkel, and my dad wrote this book for me. No, seriously. As he dropped me off at my freshman college dorm in August 2015, he handed me a leather-bound, handwritten copy of this very book. Over the course of my senior year of high school, unbeknownst to me, he had written this guide "to navigate the little, but incredibly important, choices" I was about to face.

I was deeply touched by my father's gift, and I'd like to tell you that I devoured his wisdom immediately. But if I'm honest with you, I didn't. It's not that I didn't want to; it's just that . . . well, *college*. So that book—*this* book—sat on my desk until November. Realizing he'd probably ask me about it over the holidays, I finally cracked it open and gave it a shot.

When I first looked over the table of contents, I was torn. "Invest More, Save Less"? "Date More, Relation*shop* Less"? I love my dad and knew he only wanted the best for me, but these chapter titles seemed completely contrary to what I've always heard. If nothing else, they caught my attention—and the fact that each chapter was just a few pages long didn't hurt either (again . . . college!) As I fell into a pattern of reading a chapter here and there, I had to admit: My dad was on to something. The more I thought about each simple choice he presented in the book, the more I could see those choices play out in my life. In fact, sometimes as I was reading, I would find a chapter that spoke almost directly to a situation I was dealing with at the time. Somehow, it felt like this wasn't just a coincidence.

Now that leather-bound book is one of my prized possessions. If I were to grab only a few things in a fire, I would grab it, my computer, my dog, and probably my Harry Potter books. Obviously my copy of this book is a little different from yours. You have nice, clean lines and a carefully chosen font, while I have to suffer through terrible handwriting and embarrassing yet adorable inside jokes. But the gist of the book is still the same. We as young adults get to choose how we enter our adulthood. That choice is dependent on a thousand smaller choices that we sometimes don't even realize we're making. And those little choices, if my dad is right, might just make all the difference.

My father and I have always had a close relationship; I was always a daddy's girl. This book gave me an insight into his mind, and I'm so grateful for that. But it also provided me with valuable tools for self-reflection that led me to a greater understanding of my own mind as well. My dad's words made the process of becoming an adult just a little bit easier to manage—and I know they can do the same for you.

"Suit up."

—BARNEY STINSON, *HOW I MET YOUR MOTHER*

Hello there. I'm Hal Runkel (Hannah's dad), and I want to thank you for agreeing to at least open this book. I'm guessing someone like your parents or your school gave this to you with the hopes of you actually reading it. I know you've got a million other things to do, so I'm honored you would give these pages any attention at all. Heck, as you just read in the foreword, my own daughter took a few months before she started reading this thing, and I wrote it specifically for her!

So, while I've got you . . . Welcome to Adulthood. You may not feel like an adult, and others around you may not think of you that way for awhile, but if you're in the process of launching through high school and on to college, then you deserve a warm welcome into the world of adults. You are on a journey like no other; in many ways, it's the most important journey of your life. That's why I've written this book for you—to guide you to and through this adventurous journey. And I want to start by telling you about another book or set of books I enjoyed as a kid.

Without a doubt, my favorite books growing up were the *Choose Your Own Adventure* series. They were built around the idea of telling bedtime stories, with you, the reader, getting to choose different outcomes. After a few pages, you would get a choice as to how you wanted your character to proceed. If you wanted to go left down the hallway, turn to page 79! If right, go to page 43! Sometimes you were a private detective, other times a sea voyager, still others a mountain climber, doctor, astronaut, whatever.

There were so many books, with so many choices, the possibilities felt endless. You could even read the same book multiple times, but unlike the Harry Potter books my daughter's enjoyed 10 times each, the *CYOA* books could have different endings each time.

It was so much fun being the character in these stories and actually having some say in how the adventures turned out. For a long time, I've thought about writing a nonfiction book in that format, but Neil Patrick Harris beat me to it. As a kid, he loved the *CYOA* books so much he used the format for his recent memoir. It's called *Choose Your Own Autobiography*, and of course, it's awesome. It's structured just like the series, except in his book, you get to choose how Barney/Doogie's life turns out!

Well, since I loved the books as well, I decided to follow a similar format here. This book is all about the choices that both lead you into and will determine the course of this adventure we will call adulthood. And it will be an adventure.

Here you are, launching from the adolescent nest and soaring through high school, college, and beyond. You are headed toward a life of more freedom, and more responsibility, than you have ever known. You are about to meet people from towns and counties, and maybe even countries you've never heard of, and thus be introduced to worlds of thought and ways of thinking that are wonderfully different from your own (or your parents'). You are about to be exposed to more possibilities than you've ever entertained and more temptations than you've ever had to resist. Smile often and smile big. Adolescence is leaving you, and adulthood is beckoning. It's gonna be a wild ride.

For all those reasons, I hope, for your sake, you haven't grown up with one of those parents who keeps saying, "I can't believe my baby's all grown up!" Why? Well, first of all, eww. Second, your parents have actually been preparing for this day all along. Launching you into your own adventurous adulthood is the entire purpose of parenting, and now that the active liftoff phase is beginning, it should just feel . . . right. Yes, they will miss you dearly. And you will miss them. But you should all be thrilled you're launching. This is how it's supposed to happen.

How do I know? Well, for one, I'm a family therapist and a worldwide relationship expert, having trained parents around the globe for the last 20 year or so. More importantly, though, I'm one of those parents in the launching phase myself, and I've been consciously thinking about this day with my own two kids for quite a while now. And that's actually what led me to write this book.

A few years ago, when Hannah was 16, she came to me with a very logical question. She was taking a biology class that semester, and they'd been studying the human brain and its development. Here was her query:

"Lord and Master, Father, Sir?" (her typical reverent address)

"Yes, dear child?" (my typical gracious reply)

"This week in Bio, we learned that the human brain is not fully developed until we turn 25 years old or so."

"Yes, that's true."

"Well, if so, then why do we have to make so many life-altering choices between the ages of 18 and 24? I mean, we have to finish high school, pick a college, choose a major, and maybe even find a spouse! Shouldn't we wait until our frontal lobes are fully formed and then start choosing the life we want most?"

This was, indeed, a very logical question, and she was not the only one asking it. Her question actually reflects a growing line of thought about teenagers, young adulthood, and the family and societal structures we build around them. There are, for instance, a growing number of sociologists and parents who believe we need to modify our expectations, and change our parenting, to more accurately reflect this later brain development. What these folks believe is that we should never expect, and therefore even allow, teenagers to take full responsibility for your choices—your brains aren't fully developed. So, these folks want to protect our kids from this responsibility by extending the driver's age to at least 18 or by adding at least one, if not two, years to high school.

One prominent researcher goes so far to say that we are witnessing the discovery of a new life phase, that of the "emerging adult." After adolescence, this guy says, you will not become a "young adult" when you turn 20. No, you will then become an *emerging adult*. You won't become a young adult until the ripe old age of 30. Maybe then, after your brain has been fully developed for 5 years, we can expect you to make the more critical decisions of adulthood.

I guess none of us should be too terribly surprised by any of this. After all, Baby Boomers have been crying out for a while now that 50 is the new 40—why shouldn't 30 be the new 20?

Here's why: Protecting teenagers like you from the responsibility of making choices, until your brain fully develops, neglects how your brain develops in the first place—*by making choices.* Think about this: Did your parents wait until you could speak before they started speaking to you? Of course not. They started speaking to you in grown-up language (and sometimes, even "adult" language—I'm sure they're sorry) long before you could understand a word, and that's how you learned to speak.

Hopefully, your parents have been allowing you, and encouraging you, to make choices, and letting you taste the age-appropriate consequences of those choices, since you were a toddler. Why? Because that's how humans develop into humans, emotionally, physically, socially, and yes, brain-ally. Making choices and seeing how those choices play out in the future is literally how your body grows the trillions of neuroconnections that fully form that frontal lobe and all the rest of your brain and body.

Protecting you from choices until your brain fully develops would be like waiting till you looked in your father's direction and said, "Dad?" before he ever uttered a word in your direction. It would be like prohibiting you from playing outside until your body finished growing. If your parents had done so, they would find that your body never grew at all. Bones and tendons and muscles need impact, resistance, and even injury in order to develop into a fully functional body. In just the same way, brains and minds need choices, time limits, and even mistakes in order to develop into a fully functional human.

And that is our job as adults—to introduce you to, and instruct you for, the real-world adventure of adulthood. This is the world of making choices that impact your future, and the future of those around you, on a daily basis. We lead you in this way so that instead of feeling *protected* from the big bad world out there, you end up *prepared* for it (and maybe we can help make it a little less big and bad).

Thus, I give you this book. As the subtitle suggests, this is a small book about small choices—not the big particular choices you'll be facing over the next four-six years (college, major, internships, relationships, job), but rather the smaller, everyday decisions that actually make a much bigger difference, and will have a far greater impact, in determining your life.

As you'll see, these are not black and white, right or wrong, either/or kinds of decisions. No, unlike those choices that adults have been preaching to you your whole life (like don't start smoking cigarettes, or shooting heroin, or watching *The Bachelorette*), these choices are more nuanced, more subtle, and more complicated. The ones I'll introduce and encourage here are not that clear-cut, and because of that, most people neglect to really ever even think about them.

Going back to my daughter's original question, one of the hallmark features of the adolescent brain is that it tends toward black and white thinking. "That teacher hates me!" or "You always do that, Dad!" come to mind (things you've never said, of course). Unfortunately, a lot of adults never grow beyond this level of thinking. They forever see life in a binary way: right or wrong, good or evil, truth or lie, hot or not.

This adolescent mindset searches constantly for complete certainty about things, and beliefs, in a world that rarely delivers such absolutes. The real world is far less certain than we'd like. The real world is full of ambiguity, contextual realities, and multiple ways of looking at the same thing, depending on your perspective.

My hope is that this small guide, about the small, subtle choices you're already facing on a daily basis, can provide a helpful transition from the adolescent brain you've already developed into the young adult brain that all those big, life-altering decisions you've got in front of you need most.

As you'll see, each of these chapters will present a choice to consider. Since most of life is not black and white, each of these choices will call you to just choose *more* of one thing and *less* of another—"Create More, Critique Less," for example. In that chapter, I won't be arguing against critiquing anything ever; I'll just be encouraging you to practice being more creative than you are critical. Why? Because criticizing someone else's creation is easy, and it leaves you feeling quite negative. Creating something, however, whether it's writing a song or starting a new business or cooking a new meal, is hard, but there are few activities on earth that leave you feeling better about life or yourself.

I've written to you about 16 of these "more and less" choices, along with a conclusion, matching the 16 weeks in a college semester. You may want to read and reflect upon one of these chapters per week. Yes, I know you will be super busy with classes, socials, and binge-drinking episodes (let's hope not), so I've tried to make each chapter short enough to be read in just a few minutes.

Helping raise my daughter, Hannah, into such a delightful young woman has been a humbling, beautiful adventure for me. Until I get old and gray and dead, I will cherish the memories or watching her grow up, and I'll be thrilled at her advancement into each new life phase. Her mother and I loved her into existence; we then lovingly led her into childhood. Now, we are proud to be helping her launch into adulthood.

I hope this book helps you do the same.

CHAPTER ONE

"Your time is limited, so don't waste it living someone else's life."

−STEVE JOBS

W hen Hannah initially asked me that question about brain development and choices, she ended it with a phrase that has stuck with me: "the life you want most." There's a lot to work with in that phrase. Most significantly, it conveys the idea that A) your life is up to you and B) your most important choices will be choosing between competing desires—it's not just about what you want, it's about what you want *most*. And that's what this first chapter is all about.

Behind every "*more* of this/*less* of that" chapter in the rest of this book is the idea behind this first one. Every day, all day, you and I face a myriad of decisions, and that in and of itself can be overwhelming. When do I wake up? What do I eat? What do I wear? Who should I stalk on social media? Do I have to shower today? Who do I meet with at lunch? Who do I say no to? What about yes? What are the absolute, ironclad things that I must do today? What do I work on first?

When you're in college, for instance, more of your daily life is up to you than ever before. This will bring up both the need for prioritization and the temptations of procrastination. This first choice, presented in this first chapter, is the best strategy I've ever come across to simply and surely make all those decisions easier. And it fits perfectly with the phrase *the life you want most*.

Pursue more of what you want most and less of what you want right now. I came across this idea several years ago, when I first started my own company. I was reading the stories of some very successful entrepreneurs, and I noticed a common theme— every single success story had a beginning phase of profound delayed gratification. Actor/comedian Jim Carrey talked about forgoing sleep and saying no to friends' invitations, because in the early days, in his own words, he would "drive all night across the country in order to do my act for free." Sara Blakely, my fellow Atlantan who created Spanx, spent every dime she had, and used her apartment as her corporate office, in order to buy more underwear inventory and pay her people. She spent all of her last $5,000 to pursue this dream, only to become a billionaire in 2014. Almost every great success story begins this way, because those leaders recognized what true failure is. We truly fail whenever we abandon what we want *most* for what we want *right now*.

For instance, one of the things I want most is a healthy, fit body my wife still finds reasonably attractive. One of the things I want right now, however, is a whole box of Krispy Kreme donuts. Now, I am a grown man, with money of my own. At a cost of only $7.74, I can easily go out and buy a dozen of those glistening-with-sugar, melt-in-your-mouth bites of fried dough deliciousness. And I have. In fact, I just did. Yum.

But doing so—saying yes to that tempting thing I want right now—does not lead me to what I want most, that healthy, fit body. It actually leads me *away* from it. What I want right now very often leads me *away* from what I want most.

Here's another example: One of the things I want most is a loving relationship with both my daughter and my son, filled with mutual respect, where each of them actually seeks me out as a guide through life. Oftentimes while they were growing up, however, what I wanted right then and there was for one or both of them to shut the heck up and do what they were told. Now, as a father, with positional (and financial) authority over them, I could have done just that and "made" them behave. Sadly, I confess, I did just that a time or ten. But doing so did not lead us toward the type of relationship I crave most—it did just the opposite. So, thankfully, I didn't resort to such immature parenting very often.

One of the easiest applications of this principle can be seen in how we manage our money. We all have large things we wish to own or experience, which take more funds than we have at the moment. A nice car, for example. Or a big house. Pet tiger, anyone? However, there are also a million smaller things we want right now, from fancy food to nice clothes, from concert tickets to video games. The less we spend on those things, the more we'll have available for exotic pets.

So, what does this look like for you, to choose more of what you want most, instead of what you want right now? Does it mean denying every current desire or never enjoying the thrill of the moment? Thankfully, no. This is not a program to turn you into an ascetic monk. Those guys figured that since what they wanted most was an eternal life in Heaven, they must rid themselves of any "right now" desires for anything here on earth. But I would argue that's pursuing the *death* you want most, not the life.

What we're talking about going after is the *life* you want most, which means we're not going to focus on all the things you have to give up. Instead, I want you to focus on all the things you crave more than anything else.

One of the things Jesus, Gandhi, MLK, and many other great leaders were reportedly so good at was appealing to people's greatest desires in life—and that's what we have to focus on if we're ever going to organize, prioritize, and strategize our choices and thus our lives. And I know a tool to help identify those greatest desires.

The tool is called "thoughtful wishing." The name comes from C.S. Lewis, the guy who wrote *The Chronicles of Narnia.* He observed that most people, by the time they get to be adults, have allowed themselves to get so beaten down by life that they only think about all the things they *have* to do. To speak of what they *want* to do, to these über-serious adults, was irresponsible and the worst kind of "wishful thinking."

To Lewis, though, this was horribly misguided. He believed that God had created humans with inescapably powerful desires and that God didn't see these desires as irresponsible and in need of eradication. Instead, Lewis believed, God is in the business of freeing us from the momentary desires of the flesh and releasing us to pursue the lasting desires of the spirit. Thus, Lewis called any thoughtful examination of our truest desires the exact opposite of wishful thinking—he called it "thoughtful wishing."

What I have found, in working as a therapist for so many years, is that most adults are a little scared to talk about these desires. Most of us are a little like those "responsible" adults Lewis mentioned—we either find talking about our desires a foolish waste of time or we find it embarrassing (or sinful) to even imagine. So, the tool I use is designed to help people ease into the thought process and free them up to allow their truest desires to come out into the light.

Here's how it works: On a blank piece of paper, write "Thoughtful Wishing" at the top. Try to give yourself a quiet space and a free amount of time (at least 20 minutes or so). Go ahead and do this now; I'll wait.

Now, start a list of anything and everything you want. Whatever you do, try not to judge what comes to mind, just put it down. At this point, don't try to differentiate what you want most vs. what you want right now. Start with whatever comes to mind in the moment. List anything and everything that pops into your beautiful head. I mean it.

You want a pizza from Mellow Mushroom? (It's a chain in the Southeast, and it's awesome.) Write it down.

You want a golden retriever puppy? Write it down.

You want to fly to Seattle, drink coffee in the original Starbucks, while reading Harry Potter and watching the rain? Put it on the list. Anything you want to own, any experience you want to try, any future you want to live out, write it down.

A million dollars tax-free? Write it down.

A beautiful wedding for you and some eligible bachelor athlete like Jordan Speith? Or Mike Trout? Or perhaps you want a hot rendezvous with a Victoria's Secret model? Write it down.

Do you also want to finish a degree in English, with a minor in Business, having spent a couple of semesters abroad, all while earning a high GPA? Write that down as well.

What you'll find is that the longer you allow yourself to dream and desire, the more trivial things open the list, and the more sincere hopes—the truest desires of your heart and spirit—start to reveal themselves. And that's where the magic happens.

See, as you learn to identify the things you want most, those things near the bottom of the list, you can begin to evaluate the things you want right now—and that helps you identify the ones to which you can say yes and no.

Let's say you do want to earn that English or Business or Biology degree. That would make sense, if you're about to devote your next four years to college—it'd be good to actually get a degree. But the truth is that American college students have a terrible record of starting college but never finishing. Only 59% of those who begin a four-year-degree will graduate within six years. At most public state schools, only 19% will finish in four years. That's a lot of students out there, who started out hopeful just like you, who are now wandering through their twenties, wondering what to do with their 63 completed hours, and their $63,000 in student loans.

So, what's happened here? Obviously, we cannot say for sure what's going on with all students, but we can say this much: Most students who drop out have, without realizing it, abandoned what they wanted most—a college degree—for whatever it was they wanted right then. Perhaps they preferred partying instead of studying, or sleeping instead of going to class. Maybe they chose traveling home every weekend instead of learning to launch out on their own and found their families *needed* them to come back home, whether emotionally or financially.

Each of these are small decisions at first—a simple choice to stay out one more hour, even though you have a test in the morning, for instance—but string them together and you create a trend, and a momentum, towards failure.

Where I think most people get into trouble is in how they frame those small decisions. If you think of them as good choices (studying) vs. bad choices (partying), then you actually set yourself up to fail. Why? 'Cause that is black and white, adolescent-brain-type thinking that frames all of life into all-or-nothing scenarios. And, like we discussed in the introduction, such thinking neglects the nuanced, situational contexts of reality. It also causes us to build up resentment towards the "good" choices, since they appear to never allow us to have any fun, or eat any sweets, or splurge on any cool clothes, and we always end up rebelling against ourselves. This is why strict diets never work.

The most successful decision-makers among us all, however, are able to prioritize the partying and budget for the bingeing and strategize the studying. They are able to keep their main goal, the thing they want most, at the forefront of their desires. This enables them to occasionally choose some of what they want right now, because they choose *more* of what they want most.

So, please allow yourself to want. Want that pizza, that puppy, or that guy or girl? Just learn to weigh your wants against one another and choose activities in the present moment that lead later to more of what you want most.

This doesn't mean don't ever skip class; it just means only do it in the name of your highest aspirations. If Jordan Speith invites you to watch him at the Masters, for instance, please feel free to skip class for that. (But only if you get tickets for me as well.)

Pursue more of what you want most and less of what you want right now. The choice is yours.

➡ *Now, if you'd like to learn how peanut butter has become a threat to teenage safety everywhere, simply turn the page to the next chapter.*

➡ *If, instead, you'd like to learn why you should absolutely confront people more often, turn to chapter 8 on page 67.*

CHAPTER TWO

"For every action there is an equal and opposite reaction, plus a social media overreaction."

—ANONYMOUS

W hen I was growing up, I never knew a kid with a peanut allergy. No one had ever even heard of such a thing. But now every school in America has some sort of peanut butter panic plan. That's not what it's called, of course, but you get my meaning. Peanut allergies are such a serious issue now that we all have to be on alert. One of my daughter's friends had to change her toast preferences so she could date her boyfriend in high school. One kiss coulda killed him!

What happens is called an "anaphylactic reaction," where the body inflames itself so much it closes the trachea. Kid can't breath, so kid can die. Given all the science classes you've taken, I'm sure I'm not telling you anything you don't already know; forgive me. What you may not know is that scientists are fairly lost as to how to explain this sudden rise in food allergy reactions. Peanuts have been a huge part of the human diet for millennia. They even helped build the early American economy, especially here in my state of Georgia. But now, scores of kids across the country have to steer clear of Reese's Pieces for fear of death.

Why? In a word, reactivity.

Notice that earlier I said anaphylactic *reaction*, not anaphylactic *response*. If the body *responds* to an allergen, then it would take small steps to protect itself. White blood cells carrying helpful antibodies work to defeat the foreign invader. If the body *reacts* to the allergen, however, then watch out. It freaks out and does whatever it can to shut down the invasion—even if it kills itself in the process.

This type of bodily reactivity is increasing, with autoimmune diseases like Lupus, hepatitis, and rheumatoid arthritis all on the rise. This reactivity is also what's behind the gluten-free craze, with millions of stomachs suddenly unable to digest wheat.

Without minimizing all of the difficulties of all of the above, I would offer that an even worse kind of reactivity is also on the rise. And this is one that I'm sure you are very well aware of: *emotional reactivity*.

Don't get me wrong; people have always freaked out on each other. But I think you'd agree that in our era of instant electronic connection, people are freaking out more than ever. Quick, unthoughtful, cruel tweets. Trolls online, filling up comments pages with instant negativity. Couples breaking up because one of 'em took too long to reply to a text. ("She hasn't texted me back, and it's been over 20 minutes! She must be cheating!")

A hundred years ago, when people traveled by train or boat, the loved ones left behind would have to wait days or weeks to hear from their dearly departed. Word would finally come through a carefully written postcard or letter. And then they would, upon much reflection, craft a response letter back.

Contrast that with today. As soon as the plane touches down, people rush to whip out their phones, 'cause Heaven forbid their loved ones go one minute more without knowing if the flight went down in flames.

Yes, emotional reactivity is on the rise, and it's everywhere. It's what makes for great reality TV, that's for sure. But in true reality, it makes for pretty bad relationships. Just like when a body reacts to an allergen, people can react to a perceived threat, or slight, by choking off any future possibilities. That's the real power of reactivity—it usually creates the very outcomes you were hoping to avoid. A friend fears you're being too distant, for instance. Now, maybe you're pulling away from this person intentionally, maybe not. But your friend gets reactive and starts trying to pull you closer in (constantly texting, inviting you to all kinds of stuff, complaining about you to your mutual friends). Suddenly, you find yourself wanting to create even more distance! Your friend *reacted* to feelings of distance and thus ended up creating more distance in the process.

That's how reactivity works. Get reactive; get more of what you were reacting to. Or worse. You think a professor is treating you unfairly? Or a boss? Get in their face, or whine about it to others, and guess what? Don't be surprised if they give you a worse grade. Or fire you. Perhaps unfairly, but still.

So, does all this mean we should go through life in a cold, unresponsive way? Never replying to anything for fear of creating the very outcomes we were hoping to avoid? Absolutely not. In fact, that type of cutting yourself off from any and all stimuli is just another form of reactivity. Neither freaking out nor becoming stone cold and silent is advisable. Both are just reactions, bound to backfire. Think about it: If the body did nothing at all in *response* to an allergic threat, that could be just as destructive as an anaphylactic *reaction*. So what do we do?

Learn to respond more, and react less. What's the difference? A response is thoughtful, while a reaction is an automatic reflex. A response is careful, while a reaction is careless. A response is measured—informed by education, experience, and an estimate of its immediate and long-term effects. When we respond, rather than react, we actually communicate from our highest principles and deepest desires. Reactions, on the other hand, come straight from our most shallow anxieties and fears.

In many ways, this principle is the foundation of all that your parents and teachers have hopefully tried to teach you growing up. All along, their greatest hope for you has been that you become a "responsible" adult. I know, I know, every parent says that. But not every parent means it the way we're talking about it here. A lot of adults, when they say the word "responsible," are trying to convey the idea of doing the right thing, or doing what you're *supposed* to do. This is absolutely not what we're talking about here, because I believe "doing what you're told" is not true responsibility.

The truest meaning of responsibility is what we've been talking about here. To be responsible is to be *response + able*. You need to be *able* to make a *response*. That's why the best parents have always tried to give their children choices in almost every situation, instead of just telling them what to do all the time. Your best leaders would rather you think for yourself about a situation and choose how you want to respond, even if you end up making a "bad" decision. That way, you can learn for yourself what is best for you and for others, which is one of the central hallmarks of adulthood.

I hope I've done a good job teaching my kids this, even though I know I've reacted quite a bit too much over the years. Yes, even I, the guy who wrote the book *ScreamFree Parenting*, have lost my cool and freaked out on occasion. I remember one time right after the book came out. I lost it with Hannah and commanded her way too harshly. She ran out of the room, brought back a copy of the book, and raised it up like a shield, stating through tears, "You're not supposed to scream at me and tell me what to do!"

She was right. That was the central part of that book, and it's the central point of *this* book as well. Your life is up to you. Your daily choices are up to you. At the end of the day, that's all we have—the small choices that make up our day. Are there times to react? Absolutely. When someone yells, "Duck!" for instance. Or when someone else is in danger. Or maybe when you're instantly moved to tears by a heartbreaking story.

These are the exceptions, however. And they are not nearly as common as most people believe. Getting into a car accident, for instance, is not necessarily a time to freak out. Pause, breathe, check if you're okay, then check on any others. Receiving a bad grade is also not worthy of a freak out, nor is hearing that a friend has betrayed you behind your back. Learning to respond in these and almost all other situations, when other people are driven to react, is among the simplest ways I know to enjoy the successful relationships we all crave.

So what does this look like? Keep reading. Most of this book is about different ways to become more responsive and less reactive. I'll tell you some stories, and give you some practical examples, to flesh this out.

But still the choice, as always, is up to you.

▶ *Now, if you'd like to learn how some people are actually planets, with their own egocentric gravitational pull, turn the page to the next chapter.*

▶ *If, instead, you'd like to see why "certain" people are so repulsive, turn to chapter 11 on page 87.*

CHAPTER THREE

"The secret of being a bore is to tell everything."

–VOLTAIRE

A s you head out of your family nest, you will find yourself in numerous new social situations. These will
largely be unfamiliar settings with unfamiliar people.
It is easy, therefore, to get a little anxious. After all, you will want
to make new friends in college, at your new job, etc. This means
you want to attract people, so you can have better choices as to

whom you want to befriend. And if you want to attract people, there is one easy, but rare, choice to make.

Be like Bill.

A couple of years ago I took my whole family to the funeral of Bill Hooten. 88-years-old at the time of his passing, Bill was among the finest men I've ever known, or ever will.

Bill was a veteran of World War II and the Korean War, and then went on to be a successful journalist and businessman. He was also, by all accounts, a wonderful husband for 60+ years, and a beloved father, grandfather, and great-grandfather. But I did not know him in any of these capacities. I just knew him as Bill, a larger than life man in a frail body, who never ceased taking an interest in everyone.

That was the quality most talked about at his funeral. Bill took an interest in people. My friend Don McLaughlin said this during the eulogy: "While many people enter a room with a mentality that says, 'Here I am!' Bill seemed to always enter by finding you and claiming, 'There you are!'" And then Bill would proceed to ask you more and more questions about . . . you. He was always interested in others. You could ask him about his health, and he would give an honest answer, but then shrug it off. He really wanted to know more about you.

More and more, I am finding this to be among the most attractive qualities about a person, old or young, big or small. When a person is able to shut out their surroundings and pay close attention to you, it leaves you feeling valued. When that person then listens to you, without any agenda other than getting to know you better, you feel an attraction to that person. Their genuine interest in you, shown by their follow-up questions, creates a reciprocal desire—you find yourself more genuinely interested in them.

Unfortunately, there are not enough Bill Hootens in the world. What most of us usually experience in our conversations is not a genuine interest in one another, but rather a competition to see who has the most interesting thing to say, or who lives the more interesting life.

You've experienced this, I'm sure. Someone asks you a question, you answer (or start to answer), and you can already tell that the other person is jumping at the chance to trump your answer with his or her own. This is blatantly obvious between little kids on the playground—they simply don't yet know how else to engage in conversation. But by high school, you can quickly tell whether people are still behaving like children in this regard.

These teenage toddlers are like planets with a strong gravitational pull—get anywhere near them with a story, an opinion, or any revelation about yourself, and they'll turn that into an opportunity to tell you about them. Sometimes this is flagrant: "Oh yeah? Well, try driving five hours in the car with food poisoning!! Now that's a really bad road trip!" Other times it's more subtle: "Yeah, that's true, 'cause when I went through wisdom tooth surgery, I was SO out of it! My mother filmed me and . . . " blah, blah, blah.

Perhaps the most perplexing is when these gravitational planets are totally unaware they're doing this. You're not even quite sure that's what's going on, because their replies are not about themselves per se. These folks hear something from you, and they immediately relate your experience to someone else's they know: "Well, you know Rebecca had the same thing happen to her, but her deal was . . . " Or, "Oh, you should talk to Jesse, 'cause he knows firsthand what can happen when . . . " These subtle tractor-beam replies are very common among family members, who view their responses as the furthest thing from planetary self-absorption. After all, they're not talking about themselves, right? They're just connecting your experience to your cousin's or aunt's or whomever.

But the truth is that these gravitational globes are still talking about themselves, regardless of whether they can see it. See, what they are promoting is not the other person—they are promoting *their own connection to* that other person. They have information you don't have, and even though this knowledge may be about others, it's still a pull into their planetary orbit. That's why you leave such conversations feeling a bit frustrated; you haven't been heard—you've been used. Any information you offered was turned into a tether they could use to rope you into their orbit. That's just what conversational planets do.

Let's get back to meeting new people at college or at your new job or in a new city. The one thing you want to avoid is coming across like a planet, seeking for others to revolve around you. This is the easiest way to, paradoxically, repel people. At the same time, though, you do want to make friends and grow relationships with people who care about you. What do you do?

Commit to being more interest*ed* and less interest*ing*. Make the choice to get curious about people in general and the person in front of you in particular. Ask people questions about their favorite topic, themselves. Do it with no other agenda than to learn more about them. And when they offer an answer, resist the urge to immediately offer up something similar about yourself. Instead, ask a follow-up question. Let the person know, by your attention to their words, gestures, and facial expressions, that you are interested in them as a person. Who they are, what they say, how they say it—you genuinely find it all interesting.

Is this easy? Good night, no! Not with most people. Some folks you meet will naturally capture your fascination, 'cause they're funny or good-looking or from another country or culture. More often than not, however, you will have to work a bit to stay attentive, especially if you find yourself fending off one of the planets we spoke of earlier. When you find it extremely difficult, that usually means that this person will not be someone with whom you end up developing a friendship. And that's okay.

All of this self-restraint and curious questioning, though, takes effort, even with the naturally attractive people. But what takes even more self-restraint is resisting the urge when it is your turn to talk, to make yourself appear interest*ing*. This means pausing when it's your turn to talk and then resisting the chance to one-up what they've said. This means trying not to embellish your stories to emphasize your uniqueness. This means simply telling as much truth as you want to tell, with only as much emotion as that particular story warrants.

See, if you've done a decent job at being interes*ted*, the other person will eventually ask a return question about you. This will be the other way you can tell whether this conversation will lead to a friendship. Do they ask about you? Do they appear genuinely interested in what you have to say? Are they able to keep their attention on you as you start to speak? They do not have to ask as much about you as you do about them, for they are not reading this brilliant book! You will be able to tell, however, if they are a person or a planet.

Regardless of whether these conversations lead to lifelong friends or not, your commitment to this principle will usually put you in favor with multiple people. Especially as you do it over time. I mean, you can go through a whole semester not really revealing much about yourself at all, but have so many people think, "Hey, she's really cool!"

Interested, or interesting? The choice, as always, is up to you.

▶ *Now, if you want to see how loyalty is actually dangerous to your relationships, turn the page.*

▶ *If, instead, you want to see how people who expect too much often get exactly that, flip ahead to chapter 10 on page 81.*

CHAPTER FOUR

"He that always gives way to others
will end in having no principles of his own."

−AESOP

Ask a hundred people on the street what character values they admire most and almost all of them will eventually say "loyalty." It is universally praised as a most likable trait.

I, however, find loyalty to be overrated, as we typically understand it. Overrated and misguided. Here's why: When people are undyingly loyal to other people, that loyalty quickly becomes a double-edged sword. Yes, it can keep people closely bonded through thick and thin, but it can also keep people so close that they lose the ability to question whether that bond is good for them or anyone else.

There's a million examples of this, but let's just look at a couple. First, the Will Ferrell movie *Stepbrothers*. Yes, it's ridiculously funny when "there's so much room for activities!" and, of course, when it's pronounced "Panm." (If you haven't seen the movie, those make no sense—sorry). But in reality, the basic situation of the movie is a God-forsaken nightmare for a growing number of families.

You may know the plot—two divorced people find each other and get married. They're certainly old enough to be enjoying their empty-nester years, but they can't, because each of them has an adult-aged son who has yet to grow himself up and launch out of the house. Of course, comedy hijinks ensue as the new stepbrothers fight, become friends, and start Prestige Worldwide, the first word in entertainment management. (Again, you need to see the movie.)

Funny on screen, but not so much in real life. Here in the United States, we are actually in the middle of a growing crisis just like this, with more and more young adults living with, and living off of, their parents longer than any generation before. This isn't for lack of love, by any means. Most of these parents, now supporting their mid-20s sons and daughters, are loving, well-meaning people, who only want the best for their kids. Their mistake is not one of love, but rather one of loyalty.

See, Will Ferrell's mom is so *loyal* to her son that she continues to house him even as he takes advantage of her, her finances, and her possessions. What he's really taking advantage of is her loyalty. And she allows this every time she continues to say "yes" to him, when her gut says "no." As a therapist, I can tell you that her actions are motivated internally by her guilt from her divorce from his dad, and her need to be needed, along with her fear of being alone. But what keeps all of that churning away is the idea that weaning him off financially, and setting clear boundaries on what she will, and will not support, would feel *disloyal*.

I would agree—changing her level of support would appear to be disloyal to her son. Given his need to be launched out onto his own, though, she needs to be more loving than loyal. What this actually means is that she needs to become more loyal to her principles and less loyal to her son. Simply put, violating her gut principles about what she knows she needs to do, in order to be loyal to her son, is not actually loving.

In a similar way, this is what's behind every domestic violence situation. The victim remains loyal to the perpetrator by being disloyal to his or her own principles. Again, this is not loving to either party in the relationship.

This is also what's behind every bad friendship, and you've likely already tasted this. Any time one friend feels that, in order to be a good, loyal friend, they have to sacrifice other friendships or compromise their values, this is a toxic relationship. It's not just toxic to the self-sacrificing party; it's actually destructive to the other friend as well. How? By giving someone the impression that their behavior is actually okay—especially when they threaten unfriending you, or worse, harming themselves—if you don't support them with your "loyalty."

Be more loyal to principles and less loyal to people. In order to be truly loving and helpful, we must gain such a solid grasp on our own principles that we can clearly articulate what our gut is telling us to do. After all, if you are going to end or change a relationship pattern, it's good to know that you have a solid reason. It could look like this:

No, I will not tell our professor that you're sick again, because we both know you're not sick—you're hungover. And since I'm your friend, and I want you to stop drinking so much, I refuse to lie for you.

Or like this:

> Yes, I forgive you. I do not want to hold this over you from now on. I'm also letting you know that if your behavior does not change starting today, I will break up with you. I want you to know your behavior towards me is unacceptable and in the future, I will not accept it.

It could even look like this:

> Dad, I don't want you to come up here this week. I know you want to help me deal with this professor, but I need to fight this one on my own, regardless of what grade she ends up giving me. I don't want to communicate that I don't appreciate your help or don't still need you as my dad—I do, on both counts. But I'm willing to risk hurting your feelings on this, because I feel so strongly that handling this by myself is the right thing to do.

People who are more loyal to their principles than people, I strongly believe, have the most successful relationships possible. However, this comes with a cost: They are not usually liked by everyone. They are not usually referred to as the nicest people in the world. They may even have family members who really don't like them or openly resent them because they don't always put family above all others, and above all else, at all cost.

That's okay, because these principled folks have some pretty good role models who I believe paved a possible path for all of us to follow. I'm not sure what you believe about Buddha, or Jesus, or Malcolm X, for instance, but I don't want you to think I'm preaching here about the Buddhist, Christian, or Muslim religions; I'm absolutely not. Instead, I simply offer these three, and some of the brilliant teachings and actions reported about them, as a powerful example of the principles in this chapter.

For instance, on multiple occasions, Jesus was reported to have put his principles before people. After he turned 30, and started his traveling preaching gig, for instance, Jesus was repeatedly called disloyal for befriending drunkards, prostitutes, and enemies of his people, the Jews.

One time, a would-be disciple asked if, before he started following Jesus, he could give his recently deceased father a decent burial. "Let the dead bury the dead," came Jesus' reply. Basically, he was saying that if you are more loyal to your family than you are to the principle of following him on his mission to serve others, then you are not ready to do so.

Similarly, the only reason we even know about Buddha is because of his supposed disloyalty to his family. Rejecting a life of ease in his royal family, Siddharta Gautama left the secure walls of comfort to pursue a life of philosophical and religious wisdom.

Finally, Malcolm X was revered by the all-black Nation of Islam during the Civil Rights Movement of the 1950s and 1960s. But as he himself grew in wisdom, Malcolm began to distance himself from his leader, who Malcolm thought was violating Muslim principles. So, Malcolm left the Nation of Islam in order to broaden his work for civil rights, and this was seen as horribly "disloyal."

Of course, Jesus was eventually killed for being so loyal to his principles. As was Malcolm X, and Gandhi, and "Braveheart" William Wallace and many, many others.

So there's that.

As always, the choice is up to you.

▶ *Now, if you'd like to learn why making any decision at all is more important than making the "right" decision, keep reading onto the next page.*

▶ *If, instead, you'd prefer to learn why you need to risk your life more often, travel to chapter 9 on page 75.*

CHAPTER FIVE

"Good decisions come from experience; experience comes from making bad decisions."

—MARK TWAIN

t usually doesn't take very long to learn what the acronym "TMI" means. More often than not, it's thrown out after someone reveals a little too much about their last bowel movement or most embarrassing sexual escapade. "Too much information" is used as a defense against any such further revelations. Thankfully, it usually works.

I've come to believe, however, that we should learn to use this defense against more than just poop and sex stuff. We live in the so-called information age, a time of unprecedented access to humanity's collective knowledge. This information age has completely revolutionized how we live and move and speak and relate. It has even changed the way we think. We no longer need to retain a lot of memories or knowledge, for instance, because now we can just Google it, or access access our Facebook memories.

One unforeseen consequence of this incredible information revolution, though, is how it has affected decision-making. With unparalleled access to all the world's collective knowledge, making a bad decision is now seen as inexcusable and unforgivable. "How could you have gotten lost? Don't you use MapQuest? It's all right there on your phone!" Or, "You should've known better than to sign up for that class—didn't you see all the negative reviews of the professor online?" Or, "Dude, why'd you go eat there?!? The Yelp reviews are terrible."

It's enough to make anyone scared to make any decision at all. With all the world's information at our fingertips, it's easy to fear that no matter what we choose, it will be underinformed. And thus, no matter when we choose, it will be premature. So, we believe gathering "data" and deliberating over it again and again is the best path forward. I've known a few people like this over the years. These men and women are smart, talented, and likable. But none of them has had much professional or relational success in their lives, and now they're in their 40s and 50s. But boy, can they tell you all the pros and cons of every issue! These folks major in figuring out all the minor details you must consider before making a decision, whether it's buying a car or attending a church or choosing a lifelong mate.

This is not how truly successful people operate.

See, a little known practice of successful people is that they don't allow themselves to be paralyzed by the need for more and more information before they make a decision. Successful people have learned to decide more and deliberate less. I know this sounds counterintuitive. Successful people, after all, are the ones who make the best decisions, so it would seem the opposite is true—that these people are the ones who take their time, gather as much information as possible, and then, after deliberating over this information with wise counsel, finally decide upon the best course of action.

That is true some of the time. But not most of the time. Most of the time, successful people get just enough information to eliminate the obviously terrible choices, choose a path among the remaining options, and then learn and adapt as they go. Once they set out, they will continually adjust course, but they rarely, if ever, change their minds and go back. Unsuccessful people do just the opposite. Unsuccessful people deliberate and ruminate over a decision forever, thinking of all the possible outcomes and, then, reluctantly, make a choice. But they're still not done: Even after making the decision, they hesitate to act on it, and often they are quick to reverse course and change their minds.

What's the answer? *Decide more and deliberate less.* Make a conscious choice to be a decisive person, knowing that deciding on a course of action is not the end; it's the beginning. This is because, just like an airplane's flight plan, taking off in one direction gets you going, and then you will make helpful adjustments in the air—adjustments you couldn't have made had you stayed stuck on the tarmac. To use another metaphor, all good boat captains know you cannot steer a nonmoving ship. More important than the initial direction is just getting going in the first place.

Two tools I have found helpful in speeding up my decision-making are A) the Cost/Cost Analysis, and B) the Decision Deadline. Both can be invaluable as you seek to decide more (and learn/adjust as you move forward) and deliberate less.

The Cost/Cost Analysis is a simple exercise to help you quickly get to the gut of a decision. That is, it helps you deal with the realities of each possible path lying before you. Here's how it works: Whenever you get down to two (or three, at the most) reasonable choices, get alone in a place where you are able to think best (room, library, coffee shop, etc.), and get out a piece of paper. Make a column for each choice you're considering. Now, as dispassionately as possible, list all of the definite costs of selecting each option.

For instance, let's say you're deciding whether to quit an extracurricular activity. List in Column A all the costs of quitting that you absolutely know will happen. For instance,

If I quit the lacrosse club team,

★ I'll have less time with my friends on the team. (This is a definite cost of quitting the team. It doesn't mean I'll never see them again, but it definitely won't be the same.)

★ I won't have that regular, scheduled exercise time. (Yes, I can always find something else, but that's another definite cost.)

★ I'll have to find another exercise routine.

★ My teammates may get mad at me.

And so on. List as many known costs you can think of that come
with quitting. Then, make a similar cost list for staying on the team:

★ I'll have less time for studying. (Which I need, since I'm
   taking 18 hours!)

★ I'll have less money for other things I want to pursue.

★ I'll have to continue to put up with that mean girl.

★ I may not be able to work on that service project that
   sounds so cool.

What's difficult is resisting the urge to think of the pros as
well. But most people do just that—they list the pros and cons
of each choice. The problem with this, though, is thinking of the
pros taps into our wishful emotions, and those dreamy thoughts
have a way of blinding us to the stark reality of counting the costs.
It's not that pros are emotional and cons are not—they're both
full of both reason *and* feeling. But the truth is that we humans
do far better when, after pursuing a new path, we get surprised by
unforeseen benefits; we don't do well, however, with encounter-
ing unforeseen costs. It is usually better to know with clarity what

you're giving up—that way you're not caught off guard when those costs hit.

That's why this is a Cost/Cost Analysis—after you finish laying down the costs of each option, you have a much clearer understanding of the negatives that lie in your future. Then you can ask yourself the most critical question of the whole process—which of these losses can I live with?

What I have found helpful is to finish the lists for all options and then put the list away. Walk away from it and do something else. Go somewhere else. Just be sure to set a time in the future when you can return to the list with a fresh mind.

That brings us to the second tool I find useful, the Decision Deadline. No surprise here; it's exactly what it sounds like: a self-imposed deadline that demands that you finalize a particular path. Most decisions come with external deadlines, like the last day to switch classes, for instance. Imposing your own internal deadline, however, can have some advantages.

The best of these advantages is that it ends the back-and-forth process. Most people, when facing a dilemma, get decision fatigue after awhile. (In fact, during strategic conflicts, some negotiators will draw out the drama for a long time, hoping that the other party just gets tired of the process and opts for any decision that ends the back-and-forth.)

The other, related advantage of the Decision Deadline is that it speeds up the adjustment process. See, after we make a decision, we need some time to adjust to that new reality. "Okay, I've decided to switch to prelaw as a major. I guess that means I'm on the road to becoming a lawyer. What does that mean? What will people think of me? Especially now that I can start charging them by the hour for any of my wise advice?"

So, go back to your list of costs. You've made the list, you've set it aside, you've set a deadline to make a choice, and now you've returned to do just that. Look at the lists, with little thought to the possible benefits of each choice. Just focus on the costs. And then, ready, set, choose.

Then, don't look back. Your ship is now moving, and it's time to take the wheel and steer.

As always, the choice is yours.

➡ *Now, if you wanna know why it's better to be politically incorrect, turn over to chapter 6.*

➡ *If, instead, you wanna learn how to attract people without revealing anything about yourself, turn back to chapter 3 on page 29.*

CHAPTER SIX

"Political correctness does not legislate tolerance;
it only organizes hatred."
–JACQUES BARZUN

U ndoubtedly, you are going to get into a few arguments in college. These can be the stupid kind, like when one of your roommates eats your last Ramen Noodles package, or these arguments can be the fun kind, like battling your professor about who killed JFK. Regardless, at some point, when you are clearly identifying your precise point, someone will invoke this weak defense: "Look, that's just semantics. You're just using a different word that sounds better, but it's still the same thing." Or something like that.

Here's your comeback: "There's no such thing as semantics. Each of us chooses our words very carefully because of the unique meaning those words convey to us. An 'execution' is different from an 'assassination'—if JFK were executed, then he was killed in order to be punished. If he were assassinated, then he was killed because someone else wanted his power. There's a difference." Or something like that.

Words have particular meanings, and that's what makes them so powerful. And beautiful. With that idea in mind, I have tried to be very careful with the word choices in this chapter, starting with the title.

At first glance, any admonition to "Tolerate Less" runs the risk of upsetting tons of people, especially school administrators and professors. Tolerance is an enormous, hot button word, one that will be preached to you over and over again, unless you attend a college on the far extremes of popular discourse. On most campuses, though, tolerance has become one of higher education's highest values, on par with intellectual honesty, academic integrity, and football.

There are both practical and ethical reasons for this emphasis on tolerance.

The most practical reason is because schools are trying to attract as many quality students as possible, and in a global society that means 1) they need a diverse student body to expand their market (i.e., attract more students from more cultures) and 2) they need all these diverse students to somehow get along.

The ethical reasons are far more idealistic. Tolerance for other ideas, and for the other people that believe those ideas, lies at the root of education itself. How we learn anything is by opening our minds to new ideas, theories, and knowledge from others, both past and present. Furthermore, tolerance lies at the foundation of these United States. Some of the original colonies were formed by those seeking the freedom to practice a faith other than the state religions of Europe. That's why you read such common usage of the words "religious tolerance" in the writings of our Founding Fathers.

So, with all of that practical, ethical, and historical importance attached to the term, why in the world would I advocate you to Tolerate Less?

Because we can do better than mere tolerance. Back in the day, the term had a more neutral connotation, conveying the absence of bigotry and discrimination. And you've been raised in a world that has made great strides towards increasing such tolerance toward others. But the reason you will continue to hear so much about tolerance is because we still have a long ways to go. And I don't think what brought us here can take us there.

See, today tolerance has a few more meanings, some of which carry a patronizing, if not contemptuous, connotation. If I say, for instance, I will tolerate a certain person coming to my party, that doesn't exactly preach peace and harmony; it screams condescension instead. I am up here, above that person, but in my nobility I will graciously tolerate their presence. Here's another example: A professor doesn't agree with your position on an issue, and most of the class agrees with her. Some unruly classmate starts to get heated and begins ridiculing your point. ("You're insane if you actually believe Lee Harvey Oswald acted alone! JFK was executed by the CIA for dismantling their operations!") At that point, the professor states that university policy is one of tolerance toward others and their opinions.

Is that all she's got? Think about it: Is your great hope that someone will tolerate your position in a debate? Tolerate your inclusion in a group? Tolerate your existence as an independent thinker and believer and doer in the world?

I don't think so.

What I think you want is what we all want: appreciation. We don't just want people to endure, or suffer through, the thought of our presence. That's another connotation of the word tolerance. Instead, we want people to take the courageous effort to appreciate us as equal to others, with a right to and reason behind our particular views and expressions.

Well, if that's what we want from others, then let's follow the Golden Rule and strive to do it unto them first. Appreciate more and tolerate less. Whenever you meet new people, especially if they're different from you, don't just endure them for the sake of some university policy—go further than that! Strike up the courage and learn to appreciate them as people, and appreciate their point of view as theirs.

This doesn't mean you have to accept their point of view as equally valid as yours. It doesn't mean you have to adopt their point of view. It just means you are learning to appreciate who they are, where they are coming from, and why they hold their position in the first place. This means being responsive rather than reactive, and it's at the heart of mature adulthood.

See, I know we don't see it on television very often or demonstrate it in our political debates, but maturity is actually a beautiful thing. And mature adults are magnificent to watch in action. These are people who can entertain a new idea without feeling pressured to adopt it. These people can feel a desire without having to gratify it. And yes, these mature adults can appreciate diverse peoples and positions, and even enjoy their company, without needing anyone to agree.

I've had the extreme fortune in my life to meet several people like this. One of them is Dr. Abdel Azim Elsiddig, a Muslim Imam from Sudan, who is now a professor of Islamic Law in Chicago. Abdel was my first Muslim friend many years ago, and now we've traveled the world teaching peoples of all faiths and backgrounds to appreciate more and tolerate less. It is such a joy to watch this man earnestly seek to understand others, before ever seeking to be understood.

Another such friend in my life is the Austin-based novelist, filmmaker, and comedian Owen Egerton. He and I became close friends way back in college, and since then we've watched each other question our own thoughts and beliefs about everything. Owen is definitely no churchgoer, but I call him the most Jesus-like man I know—his appreciation of others is so admirable and always humbling to watch, and his love for those less fortunate, especially the homeless, is a model of humanitarian compassion. He doesn't just tolerate them; he strives to be more mature than that and goes further—he actually appreciates how they contribute to his life and others'.

I hope you've had such mature adults in your life so far, and I hope you strive to become one yourself. One way to begin is to appreciate more, and tolerate less. I can tell you, without much doubt, those who strive toward such maturity enjoy more love, more joy, and more fantastic life experiences than anyone who merely tolerates others.

The choice is up to you.

➡ *Now, if you'd like to read how Pac-Man can ruin your life, simply turn the page.*

➡ *If, instead, you'd like to learn how this 5'11" white dude finally managed to dunk a basketball, go over to chapter 13 on page 103.*

CHAPTER SEVEN

"The meal is not over when I'm full;
the meal is over when I hate myself."

–LOUIS C.K.

A s you no doubt have learned in your economics or history classes, we live in a consumer-based economy. At the heart of capitalism is the consumer, one who divests expendable income to consume . . . well, consumer goods.

That is the demand that creates supply, the transaction that drives production. If we don't consume, we don't exist.

I believe that's why Pac-Man was so popular when I was growing up in the 1980s. Back then, that simple little video game (simple by today's standards, that is) took over the nation. The game was in every arcade, pizza restaurant, and convenience store, and it seemed everyone wanted to get quarters just to play it. There was even a top-10 hit song about it called "Pac-Man Fever!" (Look it up on iTunes—it's positively horrific.) All this success spawned an even more successful sequel game, Ms. Pac-Man. This little lady took over the video game world, as well as popular culture—both the Mr. and Ms. even starred in a Saturday morning cartoon about their whole family! Still today, it is the most recognizable video game brand in America.

That makes sense, because in many ways Pac-Man symbolizes the essence of life in the USA. Here was this tiny yellow chomping machine, just gobbling up goods, all to the sound of loud chewing. That the game exploded in popularity during the early '80s is no coincidence. That was a time of unprecedented consumption. President Reagan enacted laws that took the regulation reins off of Wall Street, and we all went crazy—consuming everything we could get our hands on. Or our mouths on, just like Mr. and Ms. Pac-Man.

We thought this new power and freedom to consume would make us happy. Just like today. But it didn't, and it won't. Why? Because it can't. Not for long, anyway.

See, the problem with consumption is that it's easy. It's the easiest thing in the world. Eat a doughnut. Buy a toy. Watch a movie. But, as Coldplay reminds us in "Lost," the shine always wears off. That new toy gets boring, and then it gets old. So you have to buy another one. That meal gets digested, and you need another one. You finish that movie, and Netflix gives you the immediate option to queue up the next one. Like Pac-Man, we have to keep consuming in order to keep living. That's what happens when we define ourselves as consumers.

This is why some of the most miserable people I know are rich people who Pac-Man their way through life, chasing after the next bite, the next reward, and the next level of the game. The therapist in me also thinks they, like Pac-Man, have to keep running in order to escape the "ghosts" right behind them. Ghosts like critical parents with idealistic expectations or ghosts like imagined enemies out to get them or maybe ghosts like guilt, or fear, or insecurity.

But this consumption misery isn't exclusively for the rich. It's available to anyone who falls prey to the advertising world of a consumer-based economy. I recently saw a magazine that's simply called *More*. Given the ads that literally fall out from every other page, couldn't that be the name of *every* magazine? It seems as if everywhere we go, everywhere we turn, we are constantly bombarded with messages that what we constantly need is . . . more.

So, if materialistic consumerism is a recipe for never being satisfied, what's the alternative? If our consumerist economy is constantly urging us to be Pac-Man and yet pursuing life that way leaves us chasing, gobbling, and miserable, then what other options do we have?

Produce more and consume less. Think about the times you have felt best about life and about yourself. More often than not, we all feel best when we have *produced* something. When we've *created* something. When we've generated something that didn't exist before.

You cooked a meal that took planning and effort, and even the eating of it paled in comparison to the joy of creating it.

You dreamed up an event, designed the look and feel of it, and marveled at it all coming together—even though it stressed you out the whole time. Even writing (and turning in) a school essay can feel good—especially if it took persistence, dedication, and a few moments of cursing your teacher to finally get it out of your head and onto the page.

These moments, and the joy that accompanies them, are simply the magic of producing. It makes you feel alive whenever you can will something to life. It makes you feel important to impart your gifts to the world. And once you've done so, you can do something that all-consuming Pac-Men and Pac-Women cannot—rest.

See, consuming, done in excess, leaves you feeling temporarily full in body and mind, but tired and empty in spirit. You know this every time you've eaten too much or spent too much or watched too much TV. Producing, on the other hand, does the opposite—it leaves you tired in body and mind, but full in spirit.

We all know this on some level, but our advertising economy screams us into submitting to the lie—we are what we consume. And that's why Pac-Man made so much sense, especially in the spending heydays of the 1980s. Had Pac-Man been built in the '40s, he would probably have left something behind, like rivets on a new battleship. That decade was about production! (Of course, a little yellow man leaving dots behind would have looked like poop, so . . . no.)

So, produce more and consume less. Put this book down and go make something. Cook a meal. Write a note to a friend. Start a project. Don't be content to just sit and consume whatever comes your way.

One of the world's deadliest diseases in history has been tuberculosis. It's caused by somehow inhaling a very dangerous bacteria that then begins to eat away at you from the inside out. But it wasn't always called tuberculosis. For hundreds of years, it was known by another moniker: consumption. Succumbing to it was actually called "death by consumption".

Well, that disease may be all but gone these days, but the idea that our consumption may be killing us is alive and well. You don't have to be a Mr. or Mrs. Pac-Man, gobbling up every food, game, app, and credit card offered to you, only to be gobbled up by the resulting laziness, weight problems, and debt. You can be a producer instead.

The choice is yours.

➡ *Now, if you want to read how people who are scared of confrontation are usually fearless when it comes to complaining (which makes them and those around them miserable), turn the page.*

➡ *If you'd like to know how* The Bachelor *and* The Bachelorette *are actually a good model for dating in college, go to chapter 15 on page 117.*

CHAPTER EIGHT

"My core belief is that if you're complaining about
something for more than three minutes, two minutes ago
you should have done something about it."

For about 100 years, baseball has been called "America's pastime." Literally, watching or listening to baseball has been our nation's favorite way to "pass the time." While I love to watch baseball during the long, hot days of summer, I have to disagree. In my experience, America's favorite way to occupy themselves has always been, and will always be, an activity that has no season at all. It's something almost all of us do, almost all of the time (even during a baseball game).

Complaining.

We love to complain. And not just us in America. Everyone around the world loves to complain. We always have. It seems to be as natural as breathing. Whether it's about the weather or the economy, our bosses or our significant others, we humans love to complain. Just scroll through a Twitter feed or listen in on a Starbucks conversation, and you can feel it. Complaining seems to have an energy to it—people get animated when they do it; they get passionate even. Maybe that's part of why we do it—it gives us energy, emotion, even excitement. I mean, if we didn't get something from it—why else would we all do it, almost all of the time?

I actually have a theory about the two primary reasons we humans have made complaining our dominant form of communication: 1) it gives us a sense of community, and 2) it gives us something to do other than change ourselves. And these two reasons are intimately related.

Think about it: Whenever we seek to make vocal our feelings about being slighted by our supposed best friend, or being screwed over by someone in charge (be it a parent, teacher, politician, whoever), it's not like we're shouting out in the desert by ourselves. No, we complain by taking our plight to another person. Or, as is the case in social media, groups of persons. And why do we do this? In order to have these people offer us honest feedback about how best to change our situation? Heck no.

We complain to others in order to get their validation and, thus, a sense of community. "Oh, you poor thing, that sounds horrible!" can be the sweetest sounds in the world. "OMG, you're right! She did the same exact thing to me!" can sound even sweeter. This kind of validation feels so good in the moment because it helps ease our greatest fear—being truly alone. We actually have a fantastic English word to describe this complaining-ourselves-into-community phenomenon: *commiseration*. A communion of misery. Finding someone who validates or shares our complaint actually feels like creating a sense of connection with a larger community. A community of the miserable.

This is where the second reason we complain enters in. See, taking our complaints to someone else (someone other than the person we are complaining about) feels like we are actually doing something about the issue. We feel energized, validated, and connected, so it must be productive, right?

Actually, no. In fact, just the opposite. It turns out that complaining to someone else is almost always the opposite of doing something productive—truth is, it's the thing we do in order to excuse ourselves from doing something productive. See, having a complaint isn't bad in and of itself. What we do with that complaint, however, is what makes the biggest difference in our relationships. What most of us need to learn is that in order to experience the life we want most, we have to learn to *confront more and complain less.*

Now, I'll be the first to admit that confrontation is not normally pleasant. Actually, addressing your complaint to the person you have the complaint against can be very uncomfortable. It can produce the opposite immediate feelings of just complaining—instead of feeling energized, confrontation can leave you feeling exhausted. Instead of feeling connected, confrontation can leave you feeling all alone and on your own.

Sounds fantastic, eh? If such exhaustion and aloneness were a possible result, why would anyone ever choose confrontation? Good question. And here's a good answer: Because the good feelings we get from complaining are temporary and eventually leave us feeling miserable. And surrounded by equally miserable people. Learning to calmly address our complaints through authentic confrontation, however, has the opposite effect: potentially uncomfortable and lonely at first, but stronger and more genuinely connected later.

So, if we bravely choose to confront, in a way that actually leads to more genuine feelings of contentment and connection, how do we do it? Well, there are a number of ways that people will practice confrontation, but there's one way that has always seemed to me to produce the best results. In fact, my wife and I endorse this way so much we actually put it in the marriage book we wrote together. We even came up with a big, high-fallutin' name for it:

Authentic Self-Representation.

Here's how it works. In order to confront more and complain less, our practice of confrontation cannot look just like complaining, except doing it to the person's face. That has very little chance of creating the connection we crave or bringing the perpetrator to some shared understanding of our perceived slight. What does have a chance of creating those outcomes, and leaving us feeling stronger in the process, is learning to authentically represent ourselves, *regardless of how the other person responds.*

See, one of the reasons people give for not confronting someone is that it "won't do any good." What they mean is that it's a waste of breath to confront Mom about her nosiness or confront the professor about a grade or confront a friend about her gossip, because doing so won't change anything. Mom will get offended (and not change her behavior), the professor will be annoyed (and not change the grade), and the friend will get accusatory right back at you (and then go gossip about you some more).

These folks may be right: The people we confront may never change—but that's not the point of Authentic Self-Representation. And the very act of bringing up our issue does run the risk of offending the other person—but we need to remember that *we've already been offended.* If we wish to continue a relationship with this person, and grow our own self-respect, we need to calmly, and respectfully, represent ourselves.

Think of it like a lawyer at a trial. Who is representing the plaintiff in this case? You are! This is your representation, stating your case. Do you want things to change? Of course! So you stand up for yourself, and let your position be known, as a matter of self-respect. Whether the other person changes as a result of your self-representation is up to them. Whether you, as authentically as possible, let you and your case be known, is up to you.

Here's what it can look like:

> "Dad, I need to talk to you about something. I could
> be wrong about this, and I could be offending you by say-
> ing this, but I don't appreciate it when you go snooping

through my things. While I know I'm not perfect, I believe I am trustworthy, and I would hope you feel the same way."

Or this:

> "Hey _____, I could be wrong about this, so forgive me if I'm totally off base. But last night at the party, it sounded like you were making fun of me, but doing it in a mean way. I can definitely take a joke, but a couple things you said were hurtful. If you need to actually say something serious to me, then do it, but don't play it off as a cruel joke."

You don't have to say this face-to-face or even on the phone. You can even text this, and it will have the same effect (just be careful, as tone is often lost in text form—there's a reason you had to take Literature in high school). The main point to remember is that you are *not* doing this to change the other person; you are doing this to change yourself—from a complaining little snit to a self-respecting adult. Whether the other person changes is up to them.

Is this difficult? Of course. That's the real reason most people don't ever do it. We all would rather just complain.

The choice is up to you.

➠ *Now, if you'd like to pursue a life with no regrets, keep reading on the next chapter.*

➠ *If, instead, you wanna look at the difference between love and loyalty, go back to chapter 4 on page 37.*

CHAPTER NINE

"Why not go out on a limb?
That's where the fruit is."

–WILL ROGERS

ormally, when it comes to young people, the word "risk" is only used in a negative way. As in, "We don't want our teenagers engaged in risky behavior," or "Our community has far too many at-risk youth."

The reason we try to steer teenagers and young adults like yourself away from risk is because we are so afraid you'll do something you later regret. Like having premature, pregnancy-inducing, gonorrhea-inviting sex. Or engaging in reckless, careless driving that leaves at least one person forever eating through a straw.

These were certainly the risky behaviors my generation was warned about. With you guys today, however, we've added a bunch to the list—like posting a frat-party pic that now comes up every time a potential employer Googles your name or, God forbid, posting a pic of your dad that makes him look exactly as fat as he is in real life. (Sadly, the camera is not what adds 10 pounds. It's the Krispy Kremes, remember?)

Are all these behaviors risky? Of course. So are trying drugs, drinking to excess, playing around with guns, and jumping off your chimney into your pool (guilty as charged). Would you regret any and all of the consequences of these actions? Again, yes, of course. But the truth is, despite all of your parents' warnings, not all risk is to be avoided.

What all of these cautions seem to miss is that risk is not just a negative term. Even big insurance companies who stand to lose millions when their clients make big mistakes don't talk about risk *avoidance*—they talk about risk *management*. Risk is not something to be avoided at all costs; it is something to be managed. It is something to be carefully calculated, chosen, and executed.

What's better to be avoided is regret. Regret is an awful feeling. It's a nasty way of looking backward that makes you want to curse your former self and shame your current one.

The truth is that most of our regrets in life aren't about the risks we did take; most of our regrets come from the risks we didn't. There was a study done, not too long ago, of older people as they approached their deathbeds. These great old folks were asked a series of questions about their lives, their choices, their legacies, etc. When asked about the things they regretted the most, their answers were almost universally the same. Almost all of them, upon reflection, said the things they regretted the most were not the things they did; what they regretted the most were all the things they were too afraid to do.

The girl he didn't ask out.

The degree she never finished.

The investments they backed out of.

The dream career she never chased.

The things he never said to the people who mattered most.

The number one thing these near-death people regretted was, by far, not being courageous enough to live out their own true life, choosing instead to live the life others expected of them.

Here's my theory: The more that young people hear about staying away from any and all risk, the more they feel forced into one of two extremes. They either feel forced to become compliant with all of the safe, responsible warnings and thus never risk anything, ever, *or* they throw themselves and all caution to the wind and engage in all the riskiest behaviors they were warned about. These young people reason they might as well do crazy stuff, since being totally compliant all the time seems like a fate worse than death.

These total rebels may not be all wrong, though, when you think about it. Remember, the number one regret of the old and dying is living a life that feels like a lie—being so scared to risk your own unique path that you end up complying with what everyone else tells you to be.

Of course, the totally rebellious path can't be totally right either, 'cause if you're only choosing to do the very things you're being told *not* to do, you are still not fully thinking and choosing for yourself; you're just reactively choosing the opposite of what other people think you should do. Plus, doing all the riskiest behaviors greatly reduces your chances of making it to old age in the first place! (Seriosly, I still have nightmares about jumping off my chimney, but failing to make it over the concrete and into the pool.)

So, what to do? Risk more and regret less. Thoughtfully, response+ably, pursue a life of managed risk. Say no to your fear and pursue the risks that have the best chance of getting you the life you want most.

* Go up to that dream guy and introduce yourself, with calm confidence.

* Go ahead and say that clever comment that has the chance to make everyone laugh.

* Take an investment trading course, and start trading your own money.

* Wear an outfit that, regardless of what your friends say, sparks joy in your heart.

* Tell your best friend how you feel when she talks behind your back.

* Choose that crazy drama or theater elective and dare yourself to audition for a part.

Take the chance to imagine your dream job, and dream marriage, and dream adventure, and dream life, and be bold enough to go after it. Even if your parents disapprove. Even if you face some early failures. Even if it feels too "risky."

When we, your elders, are long gone, and your long life (let's hope!) comes to a close, you will be alone with all your thoughts. My hope is that those thoughts are full of fantastic, adventurous memories, not fear-induced longings for what might have been.

The choice, as always, is yours.

➼ *Now, if you'd like to enjoy a hopeful story about hope (and how it cost Hillary Clinton the 2008 election), turn the page.*

➼ *If, instead, you're interested in the enormous destructive power of unfinished business, turn to chapter 16 on page 129.*

CHAPTER TEN

*"Remember . . . hope is a good thing, maybe the best of things,
and no good thing ever dies."*

–ANDY DUFRESNE,

"THE SHAWSHANK REDEMPTION"

Hope gets a bad rap these days. People tend to think of it as a dangerous way to feel. "Don't get your hopes up," people warn us. "Don't hope for too much—that way you won't get disappointed," cynics preach.

People also tend to think of hope as a weak way to live, or work. In the 2008 US presidential election, then-Senator Barack Obama built his entire campaign on the notion of "hOpe." (The "O" was for Obama, see.) The idea filled his speeches and got spelled out on all his bumper stickers and signs. His candidacy to become the first black US President symbolized the hopes of all Americans to accomplish their dreams.

Well, in an effort to defeat Obama in the Democratic primary, Hillary Clinton decided to take Obama's symbol and use it against him. In a televised debate, while talking about the superiority of her own platform, Clinton derided Obama's by stating: "Hope is not a strategy."

This was not an original phrase. Business leaders have long used this statement in order to differentiate serious, grounded strategic planning from pie-in-the-sky projections we can only "hope" come true. I have no doubt that you will encounter this notion in your business classes.

On the surface, the phrase makes some sense. If we want to accomplish anything significant, we can't just sit back and wish it to happen. We instead need to think it through, explore the options, plan all the necessary steps. Goals, objectives, tactics, and plans—these are the tools of serious strategy.

In fact, more and more leaders will state that if we do all of these steps and put in all the hard work, then we won't even need to hope at all—we can *expect* to succeed. Expectation is now being touted as a critical ingredient to success. We hear about amazing athletes, like Tiger Woods, who have always carried with them this idea that they simply expect to win. The best of the best, we're told, have such a positive outlook, and such a clear strategy, they simply expect success. And thus, so should the rest of us.

Undoubtedly, you've already met folks like this. Fellow students, for sure. These superstars simply expect to be the best, no matter what it takes. There is no room for dreaming about it or wishing it into existence—they expect the best.

The problem with this is twofold: 1) People who expect this of themselves, and expect success from all their plans, usually don't stop there. They also tend to expect that from everyone else around them, especially those closest to them. 2) People who always expect the best tend to also believe that they deserve the best—their pedigree, confidence, planning, and hard work entitle them to success. Combine these two and not only do you end up becoming a terrible person to be around, but you also become less able to deal with life's inevitable disappointments.

Think about it: If nothing but the very best is ever good enough, then being surrounded by ordinary, imperfect humans is going to make you quite miserable, both to yourself and others. And then, when your best strategic plans don't work out and life's limitations make themselves painfully known, watch out. There's a reason that every Alcoholics Anonymous meeting is filled with people trying to let go of all their "expectations." Expecting everyone and everything to work out perfectly according to your plan has an amazing ability of driving people to drink. (Or, in Tiger Woods' case, acting out in other self-destructive ways, like compulsive sexual behavior that destroyed his marriage).

This brings us back to hope. Like expectation, hope is an attitude about the future, a way of choosing to look upon what has yet to happen. Where hope and expectation differ, however, is in their approach to certainty. People who expect success, based on their lineage, their strategy, and, more often than not, the enormous expectations placed on them by others—these folks operate with a need to know *for certain* how things will work out. "My status plus my skills plus my plan will absolutely equal victory. I know it will happen. It *has to*."

Hope sees certainty very differently. Hope is not absolutely sure of what will happen, but it longs for a positive result. It sees a successful outcome as a wonderful possibility, and it will therefore work incredibly hard to achieve it, but hope would never go as far as to predict it or depend upon it. Therefore, if it doesn't happen, hope is disappointed, but okay. Hope can be saddened, but it doesn't lose hope if success remains elusive.

When the expected doesn't come to fruition, however, the one expectant of certain success looks about as stupid as all the cults over the centuries that predicted the exact date of the end of the world (you might remember the Mayan 2012 apocalypse, which obviously didn't happen). And these expectant people feel even worse.

So hope more and expect less. Hope for the life you want most, and then call yourself to the best choices, the best plans, the best tactics to bring that hoped-for life into reality. Just be careful not to *expect* it to happen. Allow yourself the joy of being surprised by new, unforeseen outcomes, which sometimes turn out to be far better than the precise results you were hoping for. Go ahead and strategize for, and work for, things and experiences you always dreamed of, and relish in the good, positive feelings such dreaming brings.

You know how, oftentimes, the planning part of a trip or event, and all the anticipations it brings, can be just as good as the experience itself? Or even better? That's the power of hope. Hope motivates us to work hard, and believe in possibilities we couldn't possibly ever expect. And then hope floats us whenever the future turns out differently.

With her unmatched pedigree and experience, her billion-dollar team and all its fundraising, plus her impeccable planning, Hillary Clinton *expected* to win in 2008. Obama's hope turned out to be a better strategy.

So go ahead, get your hopes up.

➤ *Now, if you're curious about being more curious, turn to the next page.*

➤ *If, instead, you wanna plan for the future by investing in the future, skip over to chapter 12 on page 95.*

CHAPTER ELEVEN

"I have no special talents. I am only passionately curious."

–ALBERT EINSTEIN

I n the previous chapter, we started talking a bit about the perils of certainty. It jogged my memory of a recent article and motivated me to write a whole other chapter about it. Here goes:

At the end of his sportswriting career, Rick Reilly compiled a list of the greatest pieces of wisdom he'd picked up over the years. While many of them were brilliant, and several were laugh-out-loud funny, one statement has made a profound impact on my thinking. In nine words, Reilly crystallized a thought I'd been trying to nail down for years:

"The less you travel, the more certain you are."

I had never thought of it this clearly until Reilly said it, but now I can't help but see it: Travel loosens our grip on certainty. By inviting us to engage with other people and other cultures, travel introduces us to new ways of thinking and being. We meet people with different ideas about family, food, personal space, work, sleep, sexuality, health. . . you name it. We also encounter different practices of spirituality, different models of how to build stronger relationships, and different methods of coping with life.

This happens whether you're visiting far away places like China or even stranger places . . . like Vegas. And all these new introductions can have a profound impact on how you think about your own ways of living, inviting you to question reality as you've known it in a wonderful, humbling way. If you have even a slightly open mind, all of this travel makes it very difficult to remain absolutely certain that your country's or your religion's or your family's way is the only, right way.

Now, not everyone who travels is guaranteed to humbly question his or her own certainty. I know several folks who, like me, travel consistently for work, but they only stick to the airports and hotels, and only eat at crappy American chains—and they constantly complain about all of it. I strongly dislike these people. You probably know folks who've spanned the globe, only to come back quite petulant about how backwards, or lost, other countries are. Unfortunately, this is largely the reputation of us Americans in some parts of the world. We either don't even have passports ('cause why would we ever wanna leave the greatest country on earth?) or we carry ourselves all around the earth with a snobby air of superiority.

Thankfully, not all of us act this way, and hopefully that includes you. I hope, for your sake and the world's, that you are one curious chick, or dude. I hope you love to see new sights, learn new words, meet new people, and eat new foods (even chicken feet!). It's this curiosity that turns travel into a wonderful, humbling exercise, and it's this curiosity that prevents you from becoming a dreadful person of certainty.

In my experience, certainty is among the least attractive, most stultifying human qualities one can possess. It is a function of an adolescent brain, working hard to block the entry of any new thought that would bring colors into their black and white view of the world. People who are always certain—they're the ugly Americans traveling abroad. They're also the reactive combatants in every debate, who cannot tolerate open discussion about difficult issues; they are certain they are right and that means, if you disagree at all, you are certainly wrong. If there is one clear cause of every nasty, polarizing argument, it's certainly certainty.

Most distressingly, the area of life I see seething with the most suffocating certainty is religion. You wanna see some serious emotional reactivity, just watch the peeps in the pews whenever someone starts to question the certainty of their beliefs. What do you mean America's not a Christian nation? What do you mean we may not have a perfect, inerrant Bible? What do you mean Arab Christians worship "Allah"? (It's true.) The more *certain* people are about their particular brand of faith, the less they can tolerate you questioning it.

Unfortunately, these kinds of religious folk have a hard time even tolerating you questioning *your own* faith and letting go of your own certainty. What do you mean you no longer believe in a literal Hell? What do you mean you now support gay marriage? You're not thinking of welcoming them into the church, are you? What do you mean you think Muslims and Jews and Christians all worship the same God?!?!

Here's the tragedy of all this religious reactivity: In the name of the certainty of their faith, people are willing to violate the basic tenets of that faith in order to defend it. Religious wars are the obvious examples here, but the less obvious ones are tragic as well: rampant division within their own ranks, hate speech in the name of a loving God, and family cut-offs of those who dare to venture out into other worlds of belief.

Here's the irony of all this tragedy: Certainty is not compatible with faith itself. In fact, the two are opposites. Faith is not just the content of what you believe, it's the act of believing, of entrusting yourself to a reality you cannot see. No matter how much evidence you find, no matter how logical your religion appears, no matter how many other intelligent people share your beliefs, faith will always take . . . faith. The Christian apostle Paul said once that while here on earth, we see the reality of God very dimly at best, like through a dark piece of glass. One day we will see it all very clearly, he believed, but for now we must dare to take it all on faith.

This doesn't mean you cannot develop confidence in your faith; it just means you can't have certainty of it in a way that no longer requires . . . faith. The Book of Hebrews in the Christian New Testament says that faith is the confidence of things not seen, and the assurance of things we hope for. This means you cannot come to know God by sight—you develop sight as you choose in faith to humbly seek God's way. And the more you follow in humility, the more you feel confident in your beliefs. But this never becomes the kind of certainty that no longer requires a humble, I-can-only-see-dimly-at-best kind of trust. Such humility is the opposite of certainty. If I am certain beyond faith, then I don't need to humbly trust in it—I can know it, and prove it, and then defend it.

For the life of me, I cannot understand why so many religious people can't see this. My best guess is that we simply cannot stand the anxiety of *un*certainty. *Not knowing* is among the most difficult emotional challenges for us humans. We hate it. Especially when we're talking about ultimate realities like God and the nature of existence itself.

We also hate uncertainty, though, in just about every other area of life. We don't like *not knowing* the results of our tests (medical as well as academic). We don't like *not knowing* what somebody's feelings really are (even after they tell us). Perhaps most of all, we don't like *not knowing* what to do, which choice to make in a given situation, and what gives us the best chance to succeed. In many ways, that's why I've written this book—to help guide you to make the wisest choices in the face of life's uncertainty.

And the wisest choice I know in this regard is to be more curious, and be less certain. Give up your need to know anything for sure, and increase your curiosity to learn more about everything, with humility.

Hopefully you already do this, and I hope you can use your college experience to nurture your practice of curiosity even more:

★ Take interesting electives.

★ Go out of your way to meet new and different people.

★ Discover new music and new art.

★ Attend funky and various events, even if no one joins you.

★ Above all, travel. Go on road trips. Go on service missions. Study abroad as often and for as long as financially and academically possible.

Curious people are attractive. Curious people are adventurous and fun to be around. Curious people have good relationships, even great ones, because instead of feeling threatened by others' positions, and therefore needing them to agree with their certainties, curious people just like getting to know people better.

Curious people also have the same attitude toward themselves. Instead of judging themselves as either superior or inferior, right or wrong, curious people have an insatiable desire to discover who they really are inside and what it is they truly believe. And trust. They end up placing fewer expectations on themselves and others, they routinely welcome people of different backgrounds into their lives, and they struggle far less with depression, anxiety, and loneliness.

Get even more curious and even less certain; it really is the best way to experience the world, and live in it.

I'm certain of it.

➨ *Now, if you want to know how much $2.50 in Apple stock, bought in 1983, would be worth today, then by all means turn the page to the next chapter.*

➨ *If, instead, you're inclined to eat your way through college, go immediately to chapter 7 on page 61.*

CHAPTER TWELVE

"A nickel ain't worth a dime anymore."

−YOGI BERRA

've tried to avoid devoting more than one whole chapter to a specific area, but here we are. Brace yourself for a thousand words or so specifically about financial management. Now, there's no way I could tell you all that I'd like you to think about money in just this little chapter. Thankfully, you can also apply just about every other chapter in this book to managing your dollars. So here I just want to focus on one area of money management that doesn't get taught enough, in my not-so-humble-opinion. Not surprisingly, it gets practiced even less.

Invest more, save less. On the surface, this choice can sound confusing, or even contradictory. Aren't saving and investing the same thing? Moreover, isn't the opposite of saving . . . spending? Yes, and yes.

Yes, investing and saving are the same thing, as long as we're talking about them as something you do to prepare for the future, instead of just spending for the current moment. At the same time, investing and saving are not the same thing because investing is a form of spending, and yes, spending is the opposite of saving. That's the heart of this choice: I want you to spend more of your money on investments and less of it on just savings.

"Save your money" is a very easy, and thus popular, way of dispensing financial wisdom. You can hear that advice from just about anyone, especially when you're just launching out into adulthood. It's usually spoken to you by older folks who wish they could go back and start over. They would start over by trying to hold on to more of their money. They wished they had saved more and spent less.

But that's not the reason for their current financial regrets. The typical reason for their regrets is not because they spent too much of their money; it's because they spent too much of their money *on the wrong things.*

See, as you'll learn in your economics classes, money is not a static entity; its value is in an almost constant state of flux. In a capitalist society such as ours, in order for our economy to keep growing, this flux needs to be toward inflation. What that means is our money, necessarily, has to lose value over time. When *Star Wars Episode VI: Return of the Jedi* came out in 1983, I skipped out of school early and gleefully paid my $2.50 for a ticket. 32 years later, when *Episode VII: The Force Awakens* came out in December 2015, I gleefully paid my $15 for a ticket. (And then paid it again and again as I saw it three times in the theater. I gladly admit I'm a Star Wars dork.)

What that means is that if I had saved that $2.50 in a drawer, from 1983 until now, that $2.50 would only be worth ⅙th of a ticket today: Inflation would have decreased my "savings" by that much over time. Of course, I could have put my money into a "savings" account, instead of a drawer, as some "save your money" advocates would argue. Okay, let's say I did, and it has earned the 1% average that most savings accounts return. That $2.50 would now be worth exactly $3.44.

On the other hand, let's say I chose to invest that $2.50 back then, picking up a stock share of a computer company called Apple. What would I have now? Well over $200,000.

Obviously, that's not a fair comparison—very few investments ever pay off anywhere near the 6,000x return of Apple stock over 30 years. And also, to be fair, very few people knew back then that Apple was a worthy investment. Only Steve Jobs, of course, could have predicted that Apple would become the most valuable company in human history. Actually, when he left the company for a while in the late '80s, Apple's stock price crashed. Lots of people sold their shares at a huge loss. That's why people try to save instead of invest—they're scared of the risk.

Yes, investing is risky. Whether it's Apple stock or real estate you're buying, or whether it's a friend's new start-up or your own entrepreneurial effort you're choosing to support, investing will always carry a risk. Even bonds, which have a "guaranteed" positive rate of return, can cost you everything and then some if the guarantor goes broke.

Every investment has risk, and you can pick and choose a portfolio of both lower and higher risk investments, based on your comfort level and circumstances and goals. The higher the risk, the greater the potential return, and you should definitely work with financial advisors to help you do that picking and choosing.

What I want you to get right now is that while all investing is risky, just saving is far riskier. Allow me to say that again. Yes, investing is risky; saving is far riskier. Two main reasons: One, we've already discussed—just "saving" your money as safely as possible will always, in a world of inflation, cost you dearly over time. In America, our inflation rate averages about 1-3% a year. So, if your savings aren't earning at least that, you are literally losing money.

Here's the other reason saving is riskier than investing, and this one is far more important. Saving is a fear-based, risk-avoidant, denial-focused mentality. When we focus so much on saving, our mindset turns first to reducing our spending. "I've got to stop spending so much and start saving!" we tell ourselves (and others). So we start a program of denying ourselves anything not totally necessary so we can keep it in the bank. We restrict our eating, our clothing, our gas, whatever. We do anything to save a buck. Afraid of spending, we deny ourselves any joy.

What almost always happens next is not totally surprising: We end up rebelling against our own plans, just like we do with super-restrictive dieting. Why? Brain science, actually. If all we're thinking about is all that we *can't* spend on, all our brain concentrates on is those very things. Ever notice how enticing carbs become whenever you try to completely avoid eating carbs? Your very thoughts begin to sabotage your efforts. Same with saving. The more you focus on not spending for anything extra, your brain just thinks about all the nice, fun things you're not getting. You end up with a resentment-filled, negative mindset that makes it very hard to keep saving.

What investing does, on the other hand, is place our minds on the positive future we want most, which makes it far easier to go without in the present. Why? Because we're not going without in the present—we're actually spending (investing) money on ourselves and giving ourselves the exciting feelings of a potential investment return.

Investing is a positive, forward-looking, dream-pursuing way of spending our money. Instead of denying ourselves, we're actually spending on ourselves, reaping good feelings in the present and hopefully good returns in the future. And here's how it works best: Make it hard to undo.

Throughout time, the most successful investors have been careful to choose what, or who, they invest in. And they then make it hard to immediately access those funds so they can change their minds. You may have heard people talk about "throwing their money over a wall." That's the idea: Put your money in an investment that is not easily recaptured. In money-lingo this means money that is not very liquid. Real estate is one such option, because after you purchase a piece of property, you can't just resell it the same day and get your money back (not usually). Another option is to set up a retirement account. Designate your money as an IRA, and you can't touch it till you're old and gray, unless you wanna pay penalties that could undo any returns your money has gained.

The best method I've found to begin this practice is the 10% pay yourself first rule. This is laid out brilliantly in a quaint little fable called "The Richest Man in Babylon." The moral of the story is that if you really want to build wealth for a better future, then pay your future self 10% of everything you make now, period. Throw it over a wall so you can't get to it, put it in some long-term investments, and think about it as money that no longer belongs to you—it belongs to the future you.

I cannot tell you how much this one practice has benefitted my family, and the companies and organizations we run, over the years.

Where you begin, though, is by committing to make the choice to invest more and save less. I'm certainly not saying don't ever save up for something you want to buy—that's a form of investing, if you think about it. What I am saying is that money is meant to be spent—and the wisest among us spend it on the right things.

So count yourself among the wisest, for you are already doing this. You are already practicing this principle by choosing to invest your money, along with considerable time and effort, on your education. Statistically there has not been a consistently higher return on investment than getting an education. This is not a sacrifice of four years, it's an investment in the greatest asset you will ever own: your ability to think and work at a high level.

Congrats. As always, this choice is up to you, and so far, you are choosing very wisely.

➤ *Now, to become educated about the difference between* trying *to achieve a goal, and* training *for one instead (which is much more successful), keep reading onto the next page.*

➤ *If, instead, you really hated Pixar's* Cars 2 *skip ahead to chapter 14 on page 109.*

CHAPTER THIRTEEN

"Trying is the first step towards failure."

−HOMER SIMPSON

" **G** ive it the ol' college try," is an old, and odd, expression. I think it refers to an age when college attendance was not the norm, and those who ventured there were risking a lot by doing so. It meant leaving the family, the farm, what have you, and heading towards an uncertain time of experimentation and exploration of new things.

Another explanation of the phrase goes back to old-time baseball, when college athletes were thought of quite differently. Compared to the older pros who grew up in the system and attended the "school of hard knocks," these college boys were seen as young, naïve, and, despite their new professional status, mere amateurs. "The ol' college try" was once applied to one of these young, educated players, as he tried to catch a ball well into foul territory but missed. The phrase became synonymous with any such effort, one that has little chance of success. "No way he's gonna catch that ball, but he sure gave it the ol' college try."

Give it a shot, but don't get your hopes up. Go for it, but don't believe it'll work out. This is not just the meaning behind "the ol' college try," though. This has come to be the understanding behind any and every kind of "try."

"Okay, I'll try."

"I will try to do better . . ."

"We'll try to make the best of it."

You can easily hear the weak, half-hearted nature of such offerings. That's because "trying" is something we do when we get reactive. Reacting to pressure from others, we offer faint efforts with no hope of succeeding, only appeasing. Reacting to pressure from within ourselves, we go all out with attempts that are all effort— but no strategy.

This was the case when I was 17 or so, and I desperately wanted to dunk a basketball. I was only 5'11", but I did have some hops for a skinny white boy. I couldn't quite get high enough to dunk a regulation basketball, though. No matter how hard or how many times I tried. And I tried a lot. Over and over, I would run and hurl my body toward my goal, both literally and figuratively up, but to no avail. No matter how much I tried, I couldn't do it. And as long as I stayed reactive to this fact, I would either keep trying or quit.

Then I encountered some new wisdom from an older classmate: "Dude, you're close—all you have to do is start doing a bunch of calf raises for a while, and you'll get there."

In order to accomplish something I couldn't, I needed to start doing something I could. I needed to stop reacting to my failure and start responding instead—with a strategy. In short, I needed to train more and try less.

And that's what I did. I stopped trying to dunk for a while, and I started doing a hundred calf raises at the top of the stairs every night before bed. A couple of months later, I was consistently dunking . . . a tennis ball. Occasionally, I would try to slam something bigger, and when I failed, I would go back to training. More calf raises, which I could do, in order to eventually dunk a real basketball, which at the time I couldn't.

That's all training is—doing something you *can* do now in order to eventually accomplish something you *can't* do now. Training is strategic that way. And you've likely already experienced this in several ways. Training for a sport in high school, for example, started long before the beginning of the season. Or perhaps you went through this in order to get the score you wanted on the ACT. You tried a couple of times, going in cold, and couldn't do it. Then you started working with a tutor, and after six weeks of training, you were able to nail that score. You tried less and trained more.

What most folks fail to realize is how this choice affects so many more aspects of life than just sports or school. It also applies to our relationships as well.

I have a relative, for instance, who many years ago got married for a less than optimal reason: His girlfriend was pregnant. Sure, they liked one another, and they were both established adults, but this was not the original plan. On the fateful wedding night, in order to address the awkward misgivings, the man proclaimed to his new bride the words every new wife longs to hear:

"Well, I'll try to love you."

It shouldn't surprise you that this couple eventually divorced.

Now, I'm not suggesting this Romeo should've said, instead, "I'll *train* myself to love you." That's not a very romantic thing to say. But it can be a romantic thing to do. See, trying to be a good husband or wife or parent or friend will simply not cut it. Not when life gets messy and difficult. Our closest relationships require so much maturity, flexibility, and integrity that *trying* to be good at them is not enough.

Whenever people find out that I, the Licensed Marriage and Family Therapist and so-called relationship expert, still see my own counselor every week, they are usually surprised. "Surely *you* don't need therapy—you're the expert!" My response to their surprise is usually something like this: "Serena Williams has a swing coach. LeBron James has both a footwork and a shooting coach. They don't just *try* to be excellent; they *train* to be that way. If I want to have excellent relationships, why wouldn't I train as well?"

Am I saying that you need to start seeing a counselor on your college campus right away? No. But it probably wouldn't hurt. No doubt you've already had a taste of problematic relationships in junior high and high school; it'll only get harder as your relationships take on ever-greater importance. Getting used to talking with an older, wiser, calmer guide is a great way to train for better and better relationships. As are reading good books, going to seminars and retreats, and occasionally even reaching back out to your old man or your mom.

So, yes, you can and should *train* for your relationships. Train for other things as well. Train for managing your money. Train for excellence in your profession. Train for anything that you want to get better at. You can even train to be good in bed! (Your spouse will greatly appreciate it, believe me.) I know, I know, I'm an old man you don't know, and this is the last thing you would ever want to talk about with me. But this is actually very important. There's an old joke that sex is like pizza—even when it's bad it's good. Not true, actually. Once you've tasted Napoletana pizza in Italy, you just can't ever dine on Little Caesar's again. Same thing goes for someone training themselves to be more present, more enthusiastic, and more vulnerable in the bedroom with their mate. Okay, okay, I'll stop talking about sex. (For now.)

And I'll also stop talking about training more and trying less. You get the picture. When you're faced with something you can't do, start doing what you can. Maybe you'll even dunk a basketball one day.

I did. (Just once, but still!)

➡ *Now, in order to learn why creating is better than criticizing, turn the page over to chapter 13.*

➡ *If, instead, you'd like to make sure your next move doesn't automatically make things worse, go back to chapter 2 on page 21.*

CHAPTER FOURTEEN

"It is not the critic who counts . . .
The credit belongs to the one who is actually in the arena,
whose face is marred by dust and sweat and blood,
who strives valiantly, who errs and comes up short again and again,
but who spends himself for a worthy cause;
so that his place shall never be with those cold and timid souls
who knew neither victory nor defeat."

–TEDDY ROOSEVELT

So far, after my 44 years of existence, I have concluded that the easiest thing to do in the world is be critical of others. No doubt my family has seen me do far more than my fair share. Whether it's athletes on my favorite pro teams letting me down or drivers on the road cutting me off, my easy criticism of others has been on display far too often. For that, I apologize; the world deserves better from me.

What I wish my kids had seen, and what I'm imploring you to consider here, is more creativity and less critique. Sitting back and criticizing someone else's work is not just easy, it's amazingly lazy. It's barely more than breathing to say, "that sucks." With those few breaths, we can just dismiss someone's years of effort.

For instance, it takes a Pixar team of 400 people, laboring over four years, to create one animated feature film. But it only takes two seconds for me to blurt out how much *Cars 2* stunk. It took U2 over five years to write, rehearse, record, rewrite, and rerecord their new album, but it took just a few exhales for even lifelong fans to dismiss it with "I just like their old stuff better."

Critiquing another's work is easy, and lazy, and that's part of why we all do it with such regularity. But it's not the only reason. The other reason we criticize and critique others so routinely is worse than being lazy—it's being scared. We criticize others because, ironically, we're terrified of being criticized ourselves.

Creating something of our own and then putting it out there to be critiqued by others is hard. Really stinking hard. It takes so much courage and ingenuity to put something on paper or produce something in public—no wonder most of us shy away from it. We know how easy it is to critique others, so we know how easily our own creative efforts will be critiqued!

And that criticism can hurt. It can really sting. I spent three years, and over a hundred thousand dollars, developing the ideas and then writing the words that would eventually become my first book, *ScreamFree Parenting*. This included quitting my therapy practice and risking my whole career, and all our finances, to making that book popular and hopefully starting a movement of calmer parenting and living.

Even though the book did become a bestseller, and even though we've received thousands of thank-yous from parents around the world, I can tell you this: I remember every one-star review I've received on the Internet. I can remember every flippant dismissal I've heard over the years. "This is just common sense" is the critique many have offered. "Runkel obviously doesn't have kids, 'cause he doesn't understand the real needs of parents in the day-to-day trenches," said some others. One reviewer even called me a blowhard douchebag. Sweet!

Tina Fey, in her book *Bossypants*, has a whole chapter on actually answering her anonymous online critics with personal messages. Here's an example:

"When is Tina going to do something about that hideous scar across her cheek??"

—Sonya in Tx

Dear Sonya in Tx,

Greetings, Texan friend! (I'm assuming the "Tx" in your screen name stands for Texas and not some rare chromosomal deficiency you have. Hope I'm right about that!)

First of all, my apologies for the delayed response. I was unaware you had written until I went on tmz.com to watch some of their amazing footage of people in L.A. leaving restaurants and I stumbled upon your question.

I'm sure if you and I compare schedules we could find a time to get together and do something about this scar of mine. But the trickier question is *What* am I going to do? I would love to get your advice, actually. I'm assuming you're a physician, because you seem really knowledgeable about how the human body works. What do *you* think I should do about this hideous scar? I guess I could wear a bag on my head, but do I go with linen like the Elephant Man or a simple brown paper like the Unknown Comic? Too many choices, help!

Thank you for your time. You are a credit to Texas and Viking women both.

Yours,

Tina

P.S. Great use of double question marks, by the way. It makes you seem young.

All creators can tell you that the negative criticism hurts. And if they get big enough and bold enough, such critiques can hurt enough to tempt you to stop creating altogether.

Don't do that. Instead, create more and critique less. Create stuff like crazy, and pause before you offer any type of easy criticism. Go out of your way to create something, anything, as often as you can. Write a blog, write a song, write a sonnet. Do a craft, do a recipe, do a play! Whether it's as small as a bookmark or as big as a bookshelf or as challenging as a book itself, creating anything of your own is the hardest, best, most gratifying thing you can do. It will test your courage and bring out your inner genius, and it will make you feel more alive than doing almost anything else.

Why? Because you were born to do it. We all were. 3,000 years ago, an unknown Hebrew writer put down some words that would shape human civilization as much as any that've ever been written. In discussing our beginnings as a planet and as human beings, this Hebrew writer told a story about another Being, outside of space and time, whose thoughts and wishes were so powerful that merely expressing them created a new, material world.

When it came time to discuss this God's creation of people, this unknown author includes this profound heavenly dialogue: "Let us make man in our own image, both male and female." According to this story, you and I and everyone else ever born were crafted in the very image of the "Creator" of the world.

Regardless of what we believe religiously about the story, it curiously makes sense, therefore, that you and I would feel most alive when we reflect the image of our "Creator"—by *creating* something ourselves. Perhaps it is truly who we are and have been from the beginning, and that's why the act of creating anything feels better, deeper, and more lasting than sitting back and critiquing something ever can.

In order to pursue the life you want most, start creating more and critiquing less. Put down your red pen of criticism, and pick up anything that helps you do the hard, scary, life-affirming work of creating something of your own. Ever wanted to design a t-shirt? Write a song? Paint a self-portrait? Create a new game? Do it.

Even if someone calls you a douchebag for it.

➤ *Now, if you'd like to have someone finally tell you why serious relationships in high school are always a bad idea, go to the next page.*

➤ *If you'd like to learn how trying to make the perfect decision is actually the worst decision of all, then decide to go to chapter 5 on page 45.*

CHAPTER FIFTEEN

"Growing up, I didn't get the talk of 'Make sure boys take you on a date and treat you right.' So I was the girl who wasn't dating and would just text. At one point, I remember looking in the mirror and thinking, 'You're too pretty and cool to be treated like this.'"

—MEGHAN TRAINOR

s you may have guessed from the Introduction, I am quite the hater of *The Bachelor* and *The Bachelorette*. Wow, what a collection of insecure, validation-starved pretty-folk. And some of the girls look like they're starving for something else—food.

At the same time, as I've thought more and more about my own daughter and son launching into the young adult dating world, *The Bachelor* and *The Bachelorette* are actually growing on me. Not as a show, mind you, but as a situational dating scenario: I really like the idea of young people dating multiple people at the same time.

Now, don't get me wrong—I'm not stating that I want you to get a reputation as a "player" around campus. As you'll see throughout this chapter (and this whole book, for that matter), I do not want you to choose any path that would lead you to be thought of as manipulative, duplicitous, or a game player when it comes to romance. It wouldn't be terrible, however, if you got a reputation as a "dater."

As always, the choice is yours, but I strongly urge you to date, date, and date some more. Go out with different people concurrently, making no exclusive commitments to any of them. And like *The Bachelor* and *The Bachelorette*, don't try to hide the fact that you're doing this. All those guys & gals on the show know exactly what they're signing up for, and they even know the other suitors they're "competing" with. Well, that's a situation that's really good for you—casually dating a few different folks, slowly learning about each of them, and learning most about yourself along the way. Date more and relationshop less.

I'll explain what I mean by "relationshopping" in a bit. For now, let's talk about dating. In today's world of romance, dating is becoming a lost art. Any Internet search will land you scores of articles about the death of courtship and the dearth of one-on-one dating in the current hookup culture. All of these articles sound remarkably similar, giving the impression that the dating world is so forever altered now that it'd be crazy to expect anyone to be different.

For instance, it's supposedly crazy now to expect a guy to actually ask a girl out. That's too emotionally expensive, or too financially expensive, for anyone these days. It's now all about vague passive-aggressive texts like "it'd be fun to meet after the game," leaving the girl guessing in a maddening game of "Interested or Not Interested?" Then, when she doesn't pick up that gauntlet, she gets another pansy-boy text the next morning, "'Sup? Missed you last night."

What the heck is that? Good night, dude, grow a pair—especially if you ever expect to use anything else down there. Yes, it's scary and vulnerable to put yourself out there and ask someone out. Yes, it's expensive to pay for someone else's meal or ticket or drink. You know what else it is, buddy? Sexy. Attractive. Manly. Adult.

But it's not just the guys who seem to be avoiding dating. Girls are caught in this weird new world as well. They've been raised on messages of feminine power and equality, but it's still mixed with a lingering desire for the fairy-tale white wedding. Girls believe they can and should be bold enough to pursue what they want, and yet they're not exactly sure what it is they want just yet. Do they want a boyfriend? Do they just want to hook up? Do they still want to find The One?

What all of this speaks to is a generational trend away from dating and courtship toward one of two extremes. One of these reactive extremes is fueled by a YOLO desire to have fun and keep things casual, and the other is led by a FOMO desire to grab a matrimonial, or at least committal, opportunity when you can. On the one hand, you have the much-documented "hookup culture" throughout college campuses and beyond. On the other, you've got relationshopping. This is what I call the quest to get a boyfriend or girlfriend and get exclusive as soon as possible. Even though you're nowhere near ready to even think about marriage, you're ready to settle down with your one and only. Until it's over. And then you rush to settle down again, with your one and only. Until it's over. Then just hit repeat (more on this later).

You can see both of these extremes—hooking up and relationshopping—at work in the prevailing technological "solutions" to the modern dating dilemma. Tinder is the app of choice for the hookup world, offering a world of pick-up bars in your pocket. Swipe away till you find tonight's fresh catch. Match.com and eHarmony, meanwhile, dominate the more commitment-minded relationshoppers. These apps let you swipe away until you land the one who didn't get away.

It used to be the casual way was the domain and pursuit of men, and the marriage way belonged to women. Men wanted the quick score, and women wanted to win the whole game. While this gender tension is still there (and will probably always exist, thanks to our respective biologies), its dominant domains are now much more fluid.

On any survey on most any campus, you can find plenty of guys looking for a steady girlfriend, and plenty of girls saying they're satisfied with just hooking up. Both genders are struggling to find their way in today's technology-fueled, anxiety-ridden minefield of mating. I must say that among the many things I love about being married, not having to date anyone new is near the top of the list. My wife of 23 years and I talk about how scary and awkward and confusing that would be today.

But it can also be a ton of fun, and full of exciting possibilities to learn about others, and about yourself. I believe there is a way to maximize the heights and vistas out of today's romance landscape, while minimizing the valleys and pitfalls: Date more, relationshop less, (and never, ever hook up).

Have the courage to pursue actual dating. Go out, one-on-one, and enjoy a good time together. Then feel free to do the same thing with another person the next night. And another. If you want to feel gender equal, girls, then go Dutch when he asks you out. Or, be really brave, and ask a guy out and you pay his way. Guys, step it up and just ask. Not with your text, but with your voice. Be clear, specific, and have a plan for the evening. Then offer to pay.

There is absolutely no reason you have to get reactive and turn this into anything more than it is. You are not shopping for your next committed, long-term relationship. You are simply enjoying the company of members of the sex you find attractive, with all the fun flirting, harmless game-playing, and light emotional connections that dating can offer.

Sheryl Sandberg, one of the bigwigs at Facebook who just wrote the best-selling guide for modern women, *Lean In*, had this to say about dating:

> When looking for a life partner, my advice to women is date all of them: the bad boys, the cool boys, the commitment-phobic boys, the crazy boys. But do not marry

them. The things that make the bad boys sexy do not make them good husbands. When it comes time to settle down, find someone who wants an equal partner. Someone who thinks women should be smart, opinionated and ambitious. Someone who values fairness and expects or, even better, wants to do his share in the home. These men exist and, trust me, over time, nothing is sexier.

I've clearly told my daughter to do the same. "Hannah, go ahead and date 'em all." But like Sandberg says, don't marry them. Don't even try to "try-out" marrying them by getting into an exclusive, committed relationship with them.

I don't know where we picked up the idea that it's better to be boyfriend/girlfriend than it is to just date around. It's got to be partly based on our fundamental, innate desire for pair-bonding. Maybe for the first 99 percent of human existence it was all we needed. The reality is that for the better part of the last 20,000 years, you at 18 would already be married, and already have children. So it would make sense that, from an evolutionary biology perspective, you and your peers would gravitate towards serious, committed relationships.

But every serious advance we've made as humans has involved a huge measure of self-restraint. Remember, for that same period of time we also used slavery as an expedient means for facilitating economic growth. Now, thankfully, we've learned how to restrain ourselves, for the most part. Likewise, monogamous marriage itself is a remarkable exercise in self-restraint, and it has stabilized society for thousands of years.

Well, resisting the urge to seize upon a committed relationship right now will help stabilize your life as well. It is not only a healthier way to learn about yourself and what you really like—it's also a fantastic way to build up your ability to marry for life. Much better than the serial monogamy pattern that seems so normal. This is relationshopping, and it's giving everyone a false idea about "normal" relationship patterns. See, the "normal" pattern of getting committed to someone, then breaking up, then getting committed to someone else, then breaking up again—this has a nasty habit of ingraining in our minds that there's a normal lifecycle of committed relationships—one which always ends with breaking up.

This brings up two questions:

1. If every relationship you've ever had, starting in high school, has started with excitement, transitioned into commitment, formed a comfortable routine, and then eventually died out, how are you supposed to then KNOW which one is THE ONE? Because it *doesn't* end in a break

up? In what amount of time? How long does this one have to last before you decide to make it your last one?

2. If that's the pattern you've become accustomed to, then what are you going to do, after you're married, when that relationship starts to move into the "comfortable routine" phase? If your experience tells you it's now time to break up, how are you going to go against that tradition and keep it going instead? (I can tell you, this is the situation of the vast majority of couples who go to counseling).

If you want your eventual marriage to last, and thrive while doing so, then I've got a radical idea: don't dive into a committed relationship until you're willing to be engaged. Not willing as a freshman in college? (Good. Probably not the best idea). Then don't even think about turning a date into a boyfriend or girlfriend. Don't know if you're willing to get engaged while still in college? Then don't try to snare that great guy or gal just yet. Keep dating. Yes, go on second or third dates with the same person, but resist the urge to commit to a relationship until you're willing to commit to an engagement. That way you won't be committing yourself to a relationship that's got to last a lonnng time, until both of you are ready enough to commit forever.

I know this sounds crazy, especially if you've been raised in a religious environment. We've been taught that dating around is an unholy thing to do—that somehow committed, exclusive relationships are a more Godly form of pre-marital romance. Is this because we think having a steady boyfriend or girlfriend might reduce the chances you'll have premarital sex? That's laughable. We all know that having a steady relationship significantly *increases* the chances of doing the deed. Maybe we think it might reduce the number of your sexual partners to one? Or at least might make us parents feel better that at least you're having premarital sex with someone you love?

Perhaps what all parents fear most, for that matter, is that our kids will become sexually promiscuous. We just don't want you hooking up all the time. We've read all the articles, and heard all the news about the college (and high school!) hookup culture, and it's got us reactively freaking out all over the place.

Indeed, the hookup culture is scary for us parents to even conceive. Of course, casual sex hookups have been around for decades now, especially on college campuses. But with the growing trends away from marriage, the growing power of women to celebrate their own sexuality, and the growing reach of social media technology, the hookup culture of today's youth is indeed something different.

What I've come to believe is that hooking up has grown in direct reaction to relationshopping. If there's a felt pressure toward the committed relationship merry-go-round, then of course there's going to be a growing pressure to the opposite—the casual hookup. The booty call. The one-night-stand. The friend with benefits. We call it by all these euphemisms because we want to minimize what it really is: two children playing with grown-up body parts. Two people using each other to taste the benefits of adulthood without the requirements. All the while hoping to avoid the consequences. I know I sound ridiculously old-fashioned, but hear me out.

What we should really call hooking up is "playing with fire." For a long time, I've thought the best metaphor for human sexuality is that of fire. In and of itself, fire is essentially good and a necessary element for human survival. In the right context, within the proper constraints, it cooks our food, warms our bodies, and powers our machines. We cannot live without it. Outside of that context, however, fire is powerfully destructive. Forest fires, chemical explosions, lightning—fire is among the most destructive forces in the world.

Sex is the same way. Sex, I believe, is inherently good. In the right context, sexuality has the capability to connect human beings in the most intimate way possible, bonding them for life.

And speaking of, sex has the power to create life itself! Every single one of us is the product of a sexual connection. Like fire, however, sex outside of the right constraints (a lifelong, committed relationship), sex has an immense power to destroy lives. Rape, molestation, disease, death, unwanted pregnancies, abortions—sex is, like fire, among the most powerfully destructive forces in the world.

That's why "hooking up" should be called "playing with fire." And thus, here's all I've got to say: Just don't do it. I'm not going to tell you it's immoral or sinful or shameful. I'm just gonna tell you it's not wise. Hooking up is the epitome of neglecting what you want *most* for what you want *right now*—except the outcomes are a lot worse than a Krispy Kreme doughnut hangover. I don't think it's an accident sex comes with enormous risks—it's as if sex were *designed* that way. It's also not an accident that, along with casual hooking up on college campuses, both binge-drinking and sexual assault have skyrocketed as well. They all go together like a Molotov Cocktail.

Here's a radical idea: Why not date around without having sex? Is that too crazy an idea? Probably. But even *The Bachelor* and *The Bachelorette* peeps aren't supposed to be shagging—they're supposed to be dating! Shagging is for making love and making babies, both of which require incredible maturity and commitment. Dating just requires a little bit of wise judgment, a willingness to be a little vulnerable, and the self-restraint to just enjoy the evening . . . and then go home to your own bed.

Date more, relationshop less, and never hook up. I know I sound like a crazy old fool, out of touch with the times. That's okay, 'cause the choice for your romantic life is not up to me; it's up to you.

➡️ *Now, if you'd like to learn how the excitement of starting something pales in comparison to the satisfaction of finishing it, keep reading on to the next page.*

➡️ *If, instead, you'd like to explore what's actually better than a tolerant society, go back to chapter 6 and page 53.*

CHAPTER SIXTEEN

"To finish first, you must first finish."

−RICK MEARS

F or my whole career, and for most of my life, I have been called an idea guy. That means I'm the type of person who is always coming up with new ideas for projects, services, books, whatever.

Depending on who's doing the labeling, this "idea guy" label can either be a compliment or an insult. As a compliment, "idea guy" refers to someone who's got vision—the ability to create a picture in people's minds of a new possibility that currently doesn't exist. Every new venture needs a person with such vision. "Idea guy" becomes an insult, however, when what's needed is not a new beginning, but rather a definite ending. Whenever some hot new project finally just needs to get done, "idea guy" is the last person you need around. At that point the label refers to a dreamer, with his head in the clouds, who simply cannot be counted on to bring his once great idea to completion.

Okay, I admit it. Guilty as charged.

My wife, on the other hand, has a different set of skills. As my kids know—by her constant efforts to "help" them clean out their rooms, and declutter their closets, and help them get "organized"—their mom is a finisher. Simply put, their mom likes to get stuff done. When she walks through the house, her vision must resemble the Terminator's, 'cause she scans through every room she enters, and her sensors automatically detect any and all unfinished projects. If there's stuff on the stairs, if there's a dish in the sink, if there's a dripping faucet in the bathroom, or if there's a single open cabinet door anywhere, Mominator sees it. And it drives her mad.

This is because whatever unfinished business she sees in the house, she automatically adds to whatever she's left undone at work—papers to grade, parents to call back, administration meetings to schedule (she teaches high school). Each of these things is like an open, undressed wound, and in her mind tending to it as quickly as possible is the only logical and loving response (and the only way to maintain her sanity).

This is not because my wife has a diagnosable case of OCD. She just recognizes how wonderful it feels to get something finished. Truth is, so do I. People ask me if I love writing, and I always tell them the truth: No, I actually don't like it at all. But I keep doing it because I absolutely love *having written*. There is simply no feeling that can compare to finally finishing a huge writing project, one that started as just a cool "idea" a few years back.

Even still, I am much more comfortable getting new things started than I am bringing those things all the way through to completion. Take this book, for instance. I've been thinking about and talking about the idea for this book for a couple of years now. And talking about these ideas has gotten me, and others, excited and energized, as all good ideas and good starts tend to do. But eventually, I actually have to write it. I actually have to sit down, shut out all the distractions that become so much more enticing (squirrel!), and finish the darn thing.

Finishing is not my strong suit, but I love it. See, finishing is where the magic happens. I know that starting something new can feel magic, but as *Inc. Magazine* writer Jeff Haden says: "Ideas without action aren't really ideas; they're regrets." That's why finishing something, anything, is a feeling that cannot be replicated by much else in life. That's why you need to finish more and start less.

You already know this by now. You already know the freeing, empowering feeling of completing a project or turning in a paper or maybe even walking across the stage to collect your diploma, knowing your high school work was done. Finishing has a way of producing a sense of genuine satisfaction that, again, cannot be reproduced by anything else in life.

So why don't we do it more often? If closing out our unfinished business is so freeing and satisfying, why do we tend to avoid it?

I can think of several reasons, but they all share the same theme: We avoid finishing things because finishing things is hard. Really hard. Even right now, halfway through the writing of this chapter, my mind is scrambling for something else to get started on and also scrambling for a way to rationalize whatever distraction I choose . . .

Okay, I'm back. Right after I finished that last sentence, I went and started a workout. I mean, I was already in the basement, and the bench press is just a few steps away, and don't I really need a good workout? Wouldn't that put me in a better state of mind to write? Let the procrastination justification begin!

It is so easy to avoid finishing something because finishing anything is hard. It takes guts. It takes grit. It takes discipline. It takes a willingness to work alone, because when it's absolutely time to get something finished, most people involved will find their way out and thus leave it to the finishers.

I've been told my whole life that I'm a visionary, capable of seeing things and possibilities. But all that's for nothing if I never follow through and help bring those things into reality. Starting things is cool, and I want you to continuously think about new ideas and ways for things to work.

But learning to finish, and finish well–thats the only way to truly make a difference. Yes, dare to start new things. Yes, be a dreamer and an "idea guy." But work hard at noticing your unfinished business and work hard getting it done.

➠ *Now, if you've been skipping around and have yet to read all the chapters, go ahead and do that before proceeding any further. The next chapter is the last, and most important, and it's not like any that have come before.*

➠ *It's the most important choice of all.*

"They say that nobody is perfect.
Then they tell you practice makes perfect.
I wish they'd make up their minds."

—WILT CHAMBERLAIN

Throughout this book, we've been talking about the nuanced choices of life. These are the "sometimes" choices, the contextual questions that force us out of our black and white view of the world. These are the "more of this, less of that" choices, which give us the best chance to have the adventurous adulthood we want most.

How I want to end the book is different, though. I wish to end it by presenting you with another choice to consider, but I see no nuance or context in this one—it's truly an either/or decision. And how you decide this one has the greatest impact on all the others, so I want you to consider it very carefully:

> *You can be perfect, or you can be real;*
> *You can hide, or you can heal.*

I apologize for the rhyme. I promise I didn't plan it that way; it just came out. I'm glad, though, because hopefully it makes this choice more memorable—and I really want you to remember this one.

Over the years, I've gotten to work with a good number of high-achieving families. Not all of them had great wealth, but that's only one indicator of great success. Some of these folks had multiple PhDs, worked very high up in their professions, and had a decent amount of acclaim from others. Of course, a number of these folks have had great financial success, and social status, as a result.

Usually, the reason these families end up in my office is a concern about one of their teenage or young adult children. Some of these sons and daughters were struggling with addiction, battling depression or anxiety attacks, or suffering through an eating disorder.

Still others of these launching young adults were having a hard time finding their way in adulthood, and by the time they come to see me the family is up in arms with frustration or beside themselves with worry. They don't know what they're doing wrong, and they desperately want to find an answer. They just want a fix to this problem.

At the risk of appearing insensitive, I usually ask them: "Why?"

It's not that I'm trying to be provocative; I just want to gauge how anxious or embarrassed they are about having this problem to begin with. The more they freak out at my question, the more I know: These folks *hate* being imperfect. One or more of the members of this family cannot stand having this problem, whatever it is, because they have so much invested in looking, feeling, and believing they're close to perfect.

Of course, no one admits this out loud. No one ever actually says they're perfect or their family is perfect. But you can always tell by how people react when a problem arises—especially a problem that successful people aren't supposed to struggle with: suicidal depression, for instance. Or terrifying panic attacks. One of the most popular TV shows of the last 30 years is *The*

Sopranos, built around the premise of what would happen if an Italian mafia tough guy started therapy in order to deal with his panic attacks. It made for fascinating TV.

The irony is that these particular struggles, while they can strike anyone, are particularly common in these family environments, with high expectations to perform well and shine before others. It's not accidental, for instance, that the vast majority of eating disorders occur in white, upper-class families with high visibility and pressure to appear a certain way. It's also not accidental that addictions thrive in secrecy, when the addicts, and/or their families work hard to hide their imperfections.

> *You can be perfect, or you can be real;*
> *You can hide, or you can heal.*

For as long as we humans have lived in community, we have struggled with what to do with our struggles. It doesn't take being wealthy or successful to give in to our first instinct—we all want to hide our less-than-perfect lives. This is the instinct I want you to resist most, though. It's not easy, by any means, but none of these choices are. And none are more important than this one.

The reality is that any struggle, whether it be with anxiety or asthma, depression or diabetes, doesn't actually separate us from everyone else. We all have struggles, so being open about our own actually *increases* our chances of uniting us with others. Especially the others that we actually would want to unite with. And that's what you really want most.

You are gonna have moments, and even seasons, when you struggle. These may be times of doubt or crises of confidence or serious emotional issues. You may have health concerns, you may develop depression, or you may really wreck your romantic relationship. None of these should scare you. Life is difficult, and our struggles give us the opportunity to grow stronger, and more human at the same time. What should scare you is any effort you make to hide these struggles, because that does just the opposite: Hiding makes you weaker and less human at the same time.

Truth is, there is no reason to hide. Everyone you meet is, at some level, full of it. Everyone is, at one point or another, full of inconsistency, full of hypocrisy, and full of the ability to judge others for the very same thing they themselves struggle with. Hypocrisy and duplicity about our struggles is as common as our struggles themselves. This is, obviously, why it's important to be open about yours. Nothing invites struggles to become full-blown problems like duplicity, pretense, and secrecy.

But I don't want you to be open to just anyone and everyone. Everyone is full of it, but not everyone is strong, and human, enough to be aware of it. And not everyone is capable of, or interested in, being discreet and trustworthy with your precious confessions. These people are not to be trusted, and you should keep them at arms length at best, if you want to pursue the life you want most.

In contrast, the very best people are aware of our their fallacies, and aren't terrified to have someone point them out. These are the ones who can admit their imperfections and welcome others' feedback. These are the people to seek out. These are the people to be friends with, to take on the world with, and to partner your whole life with. When you inevitably struggle, these are the people to open up to. Invite these folks in. Share your scares with them. Reach out to these fellow imperfects and be vulnerable, honest, broken, and real.

If you pay attention to only one of all these choices, may it please be this one. I promise that the more you lead with your vulnerability, the more you're honest about your imperfections, the more you'll grow stronger through those inevitable seasons of struggle, and the less you'll ever feel truly alone.

You can be perfect or you can be real. You can hide or you can heal.

As always, the choice is yours.

ACKNOWLEDGMENTS

There are several I need to thank for making this book a reality:

* My home team, which gives me the greatest advantage in life: Hannah and Brandon, the two fantastic young adults I get the privilege of watching launch and soar on their own, and my favorite adult in the world, my lifelong mate and best friend, Jenny.

* The team at ScreamFree, especially my business partner for 12 years now, Jon Kaplan.

* Those who gave me great feedback on the manuscript: Michelle Brechbuhl, Sarah Holley, Tasha Kaplan, Don McLaughlin, and Owen Egerton.

* The education professionals who helped steer me towards the current academic and developmental issues facing our young adults: Dr. Chris Gonzalez at Lipscomb University, Dr. Eric Moschella at the University of South Carolina, Dr. Constance Relihan at Auburn University, Daniel

Cline at Legacy Community Academy, and Derek Wilson at Greater Atlanta Christian School.

* And speaking of Greater Atlanta Christian, the high school students of Mrs. Runkel's leadership rotation, who served so well as willing guinea pigs for this material. In particular, I'd like to thank Caroline Wigmore, Ryan Cameron, Ford Higgins , Will Brooks, and Joshua Pickens, but everyone's feedback was so helpful. Thanks guys!

* The board at The ScreamFree Institute, who have steered our nonprofit work through many adventures: Ken Shumard, Fernando Nasmyth, Michelle Brechbuhl, Julie Baumgardner, Dale Armstrong, Louie Werderich, and Tim Pownall

* Gary and Karen Chamblee, who graciously lent us their beautiful North Georgia mountain cabin for a writing retreat.

* The team at Greenleaf Book Group: Tanya Hall, Justin Branch, Emilie Lyons, Kat Fatland, and Kim Lance.

ABOUT THE AUTHOR

Hal Runkel is one of the world's most trusted life improvement experts. His practical wisdom on relationships, conflict, and decision-making helps thousands of people around the world find renewed peace and prosperity every day.

A Licensed Marriage and Family Therapist, registered conflict mediator, and internationally acclaimed speaker, Hal is the *New York Times* bestselling author of *ScreamFree Parenting* and *ScreamFree Marriage*. Those books have reached hundreds of thousands around the world, and have been translated into 11 languages. Hal and his ScreamFree message have been featured on over a thousand media outlets, including over 40 appearances on NBC's *Today Show*, as well as countless TV and radio stations and publications around the country.

Hal and his wife, Jenny, started dating when they were teens and have now been married for 23 years. They are constantly striving to stay calm and connected with each other and their two launching adults, Hannah (20), and Brandon(17). Hal and Jenny both consider Houston, Texas, their hometown, but since 2000 they've called Atlanta, Georgia home.